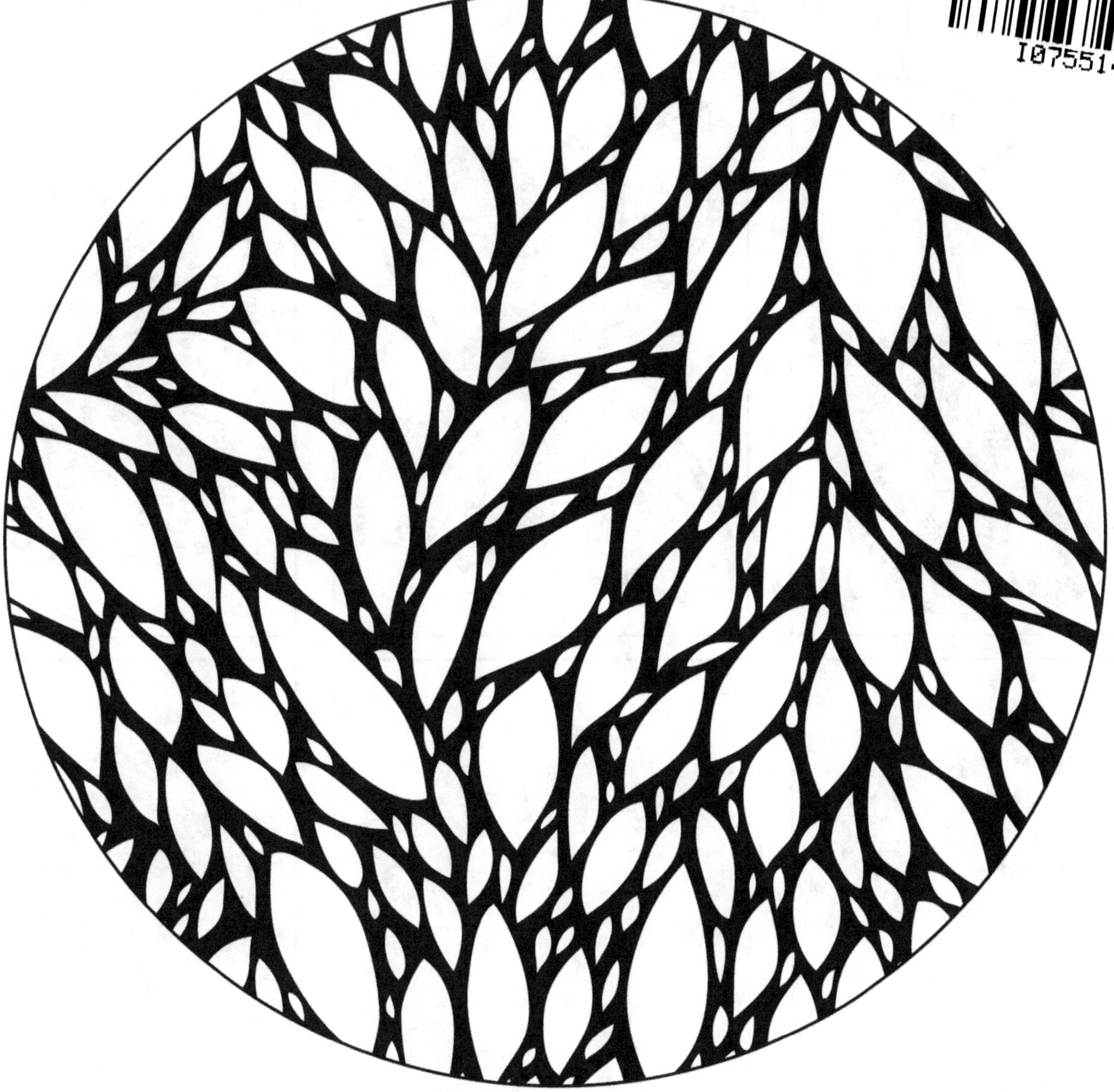

Anti-Stress Coloring Book

Nature Designs Vol 1

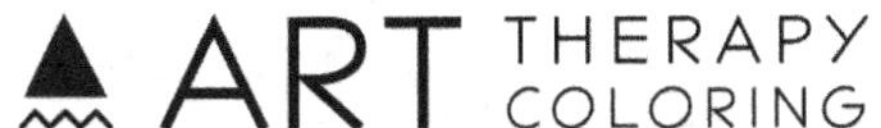

Preview of Coloring Pages

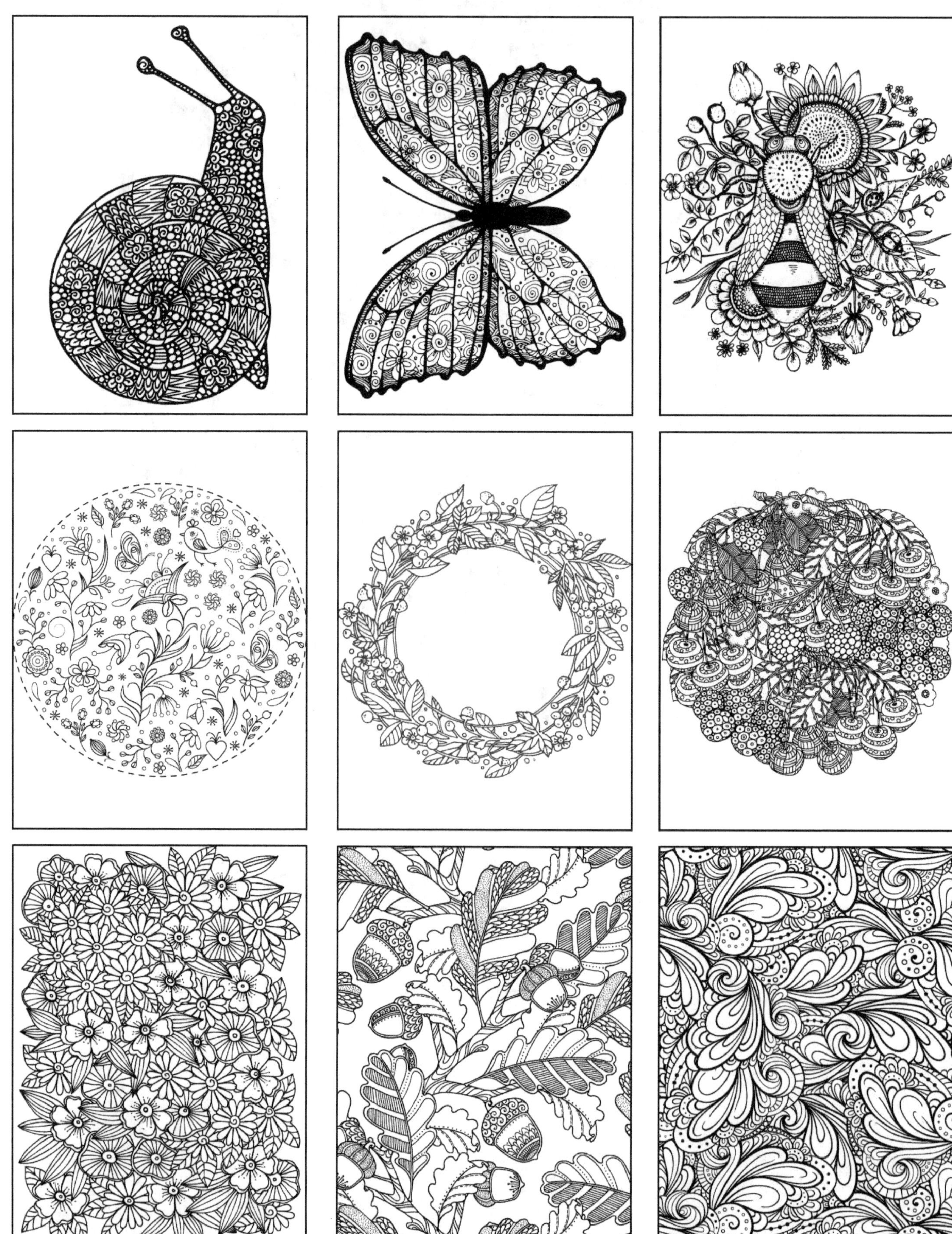

www.arttherapycoloring.com

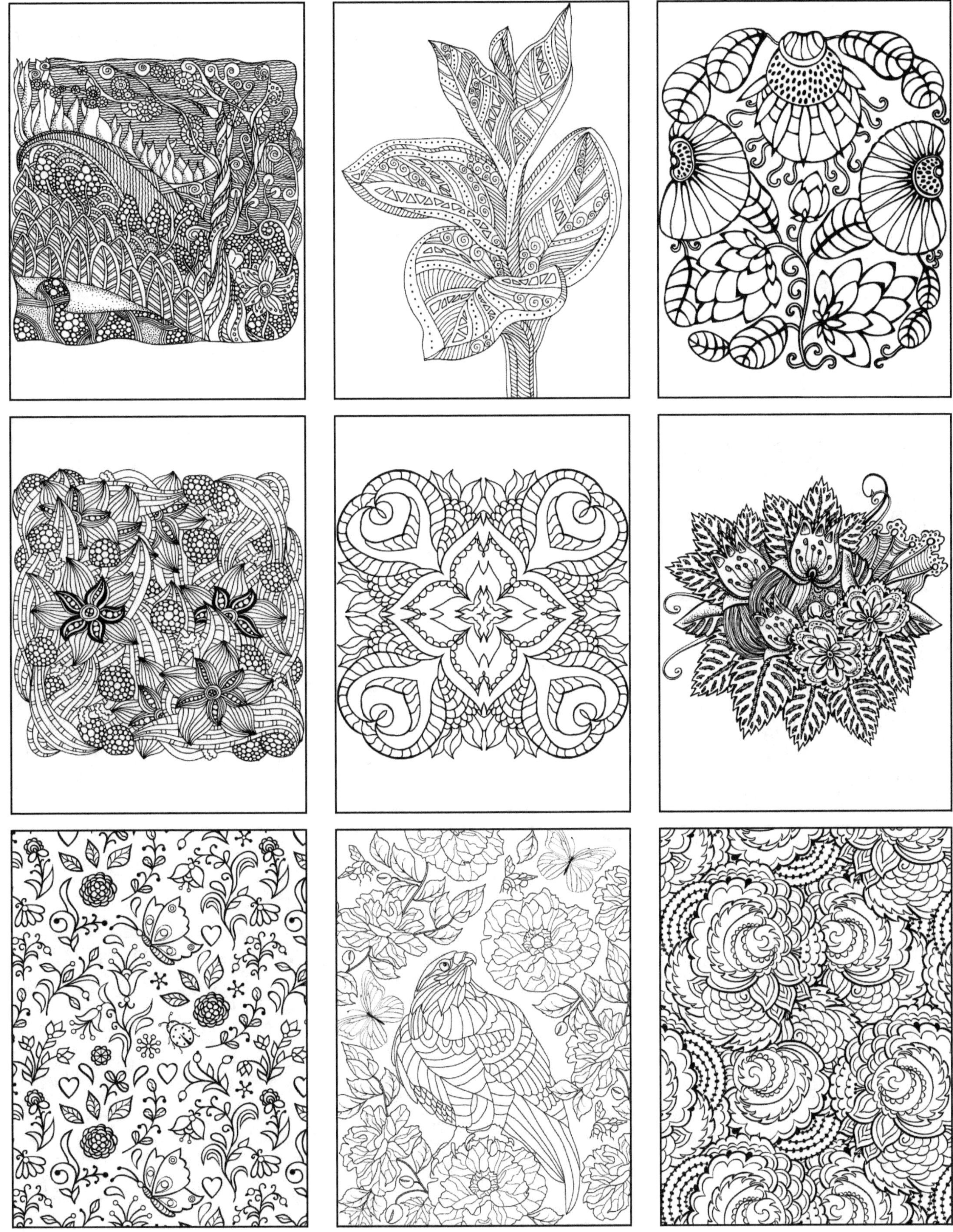

Preview of Coloring Pages

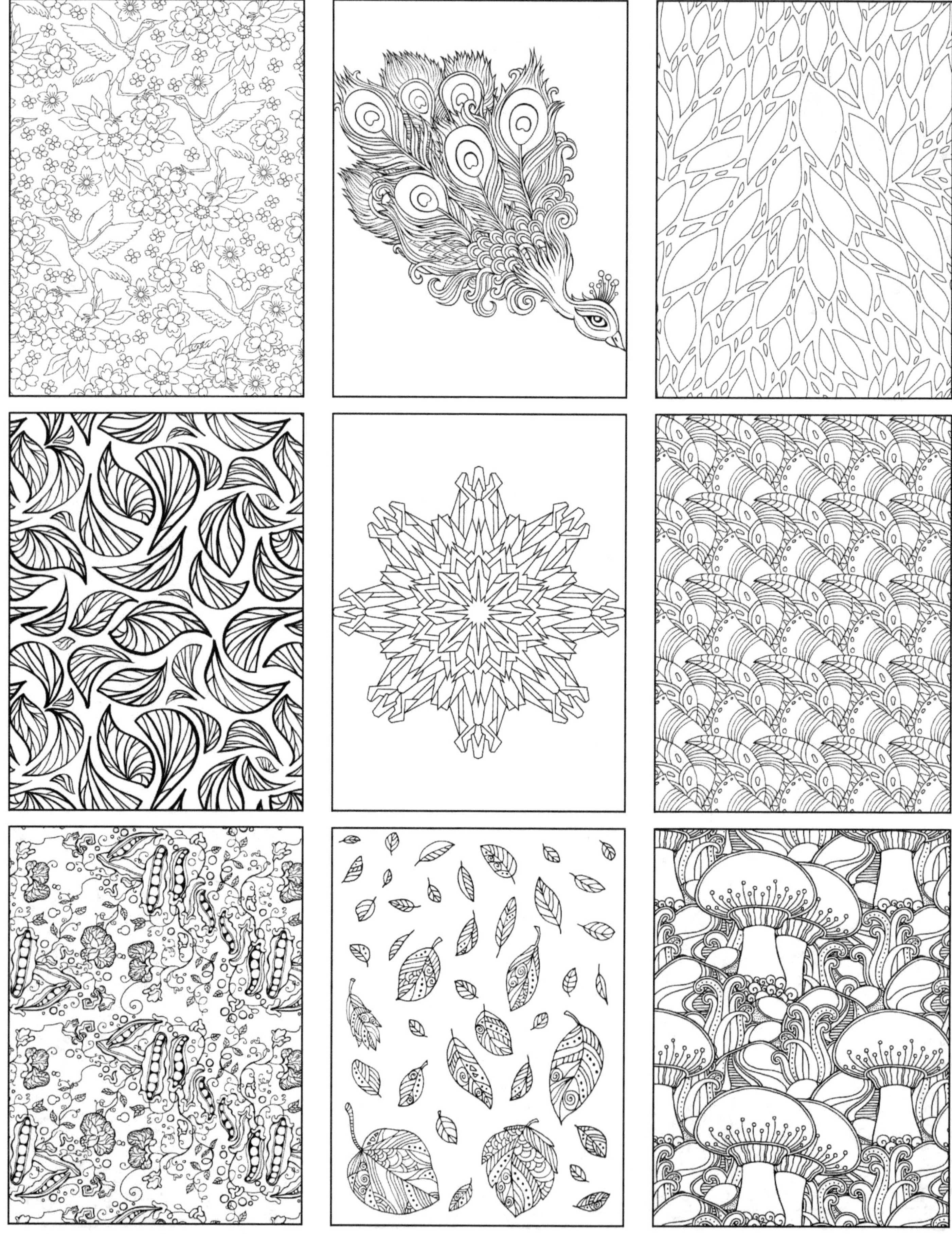

www.arttherapycoloring.com

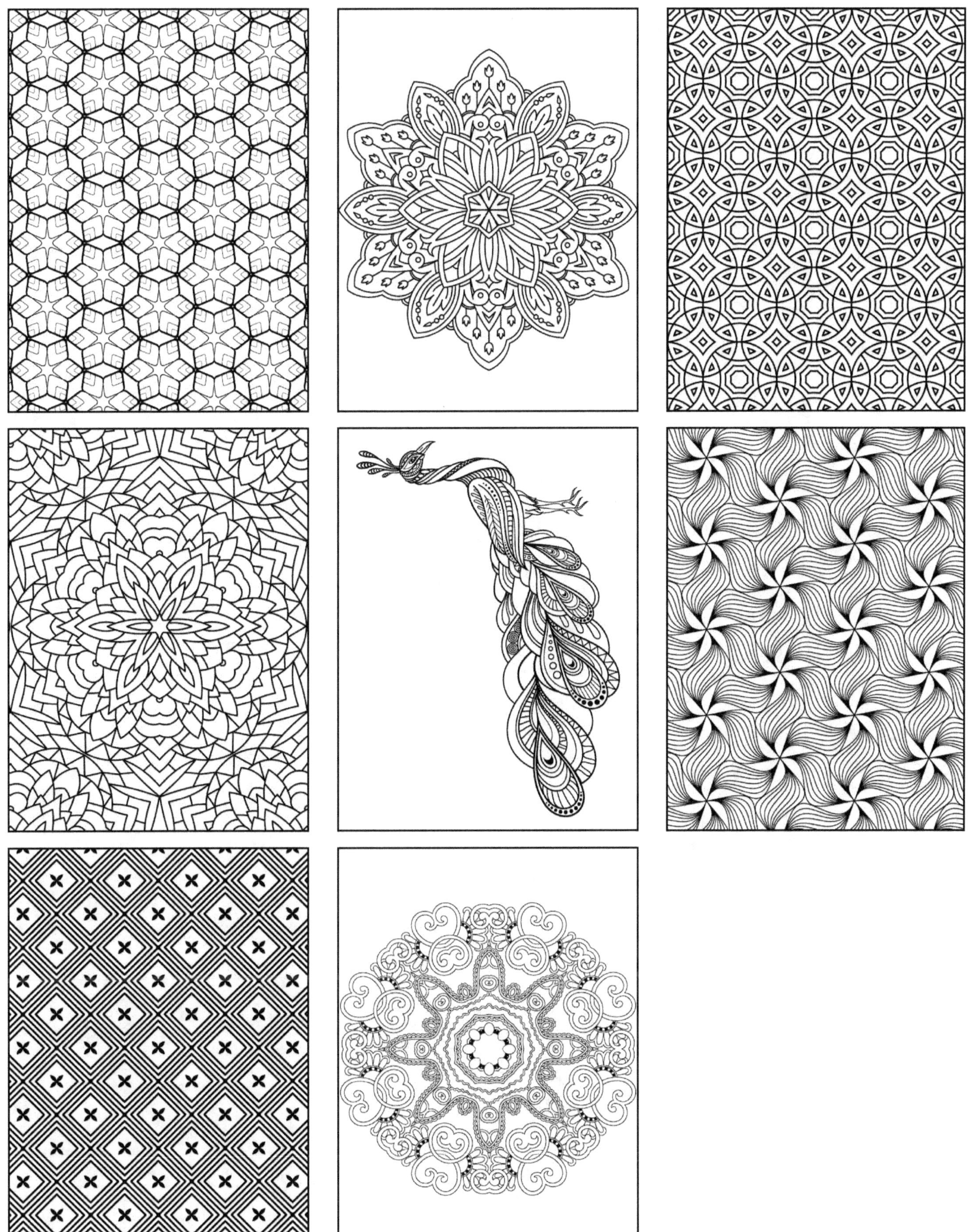

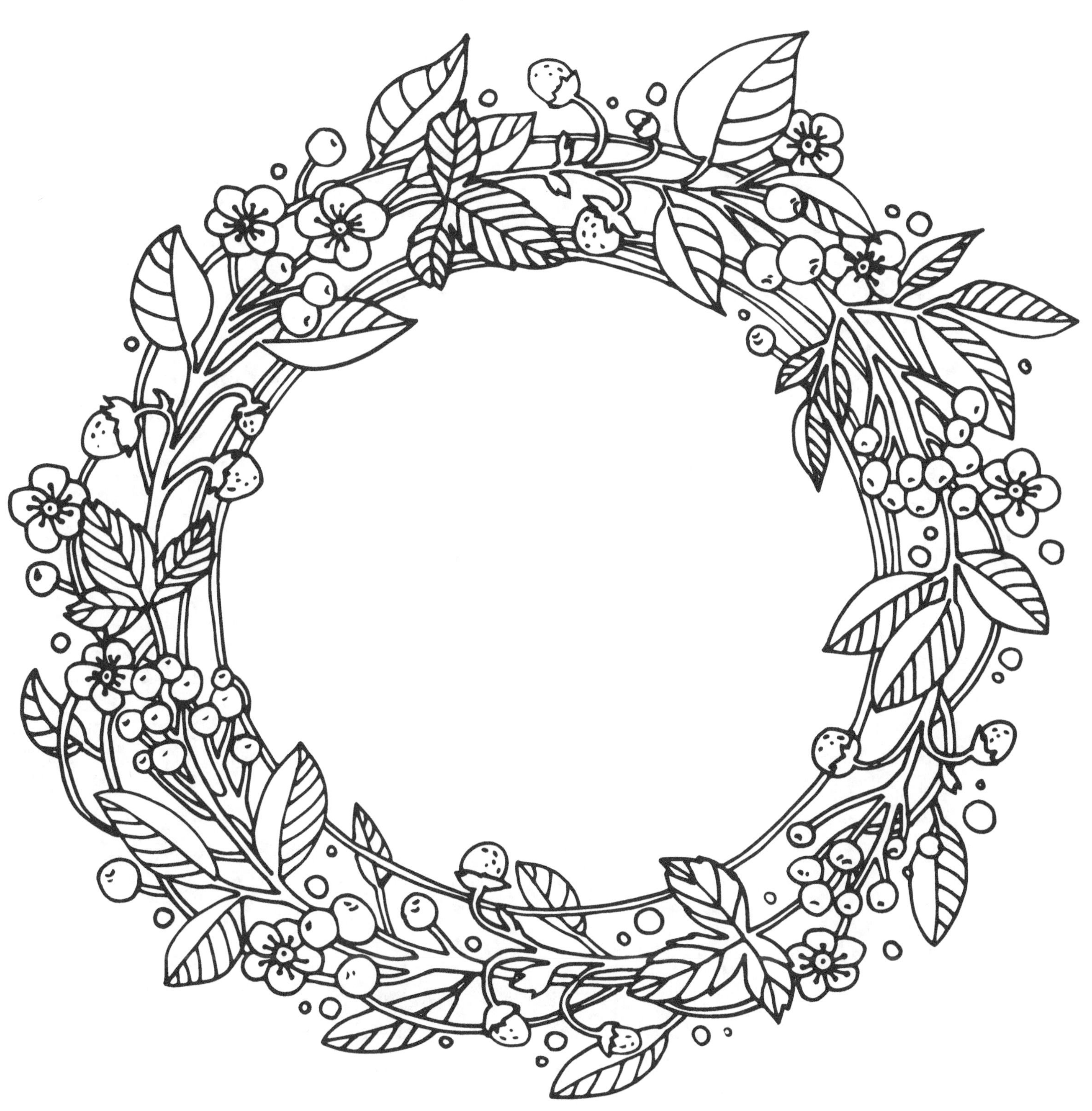

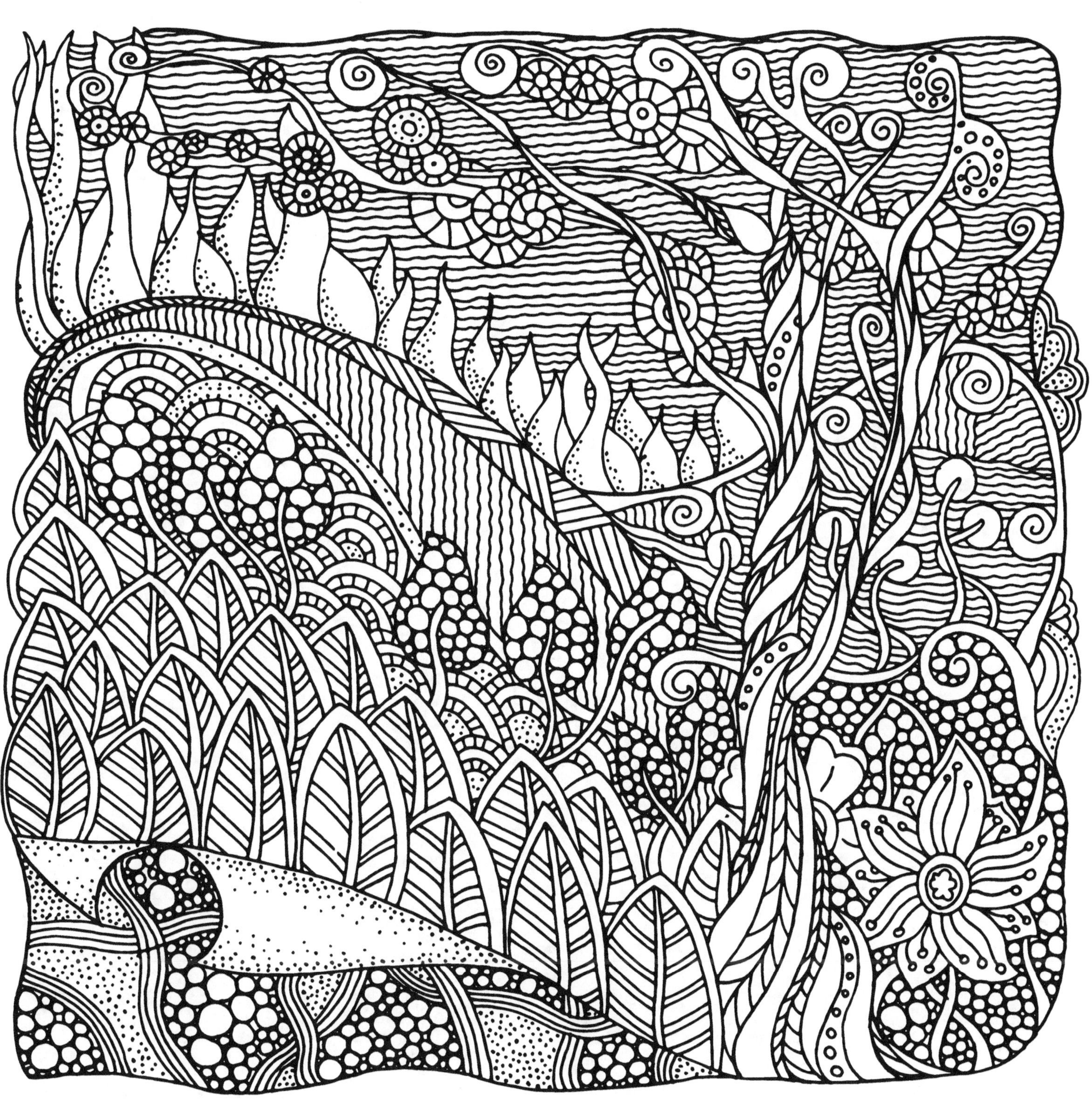

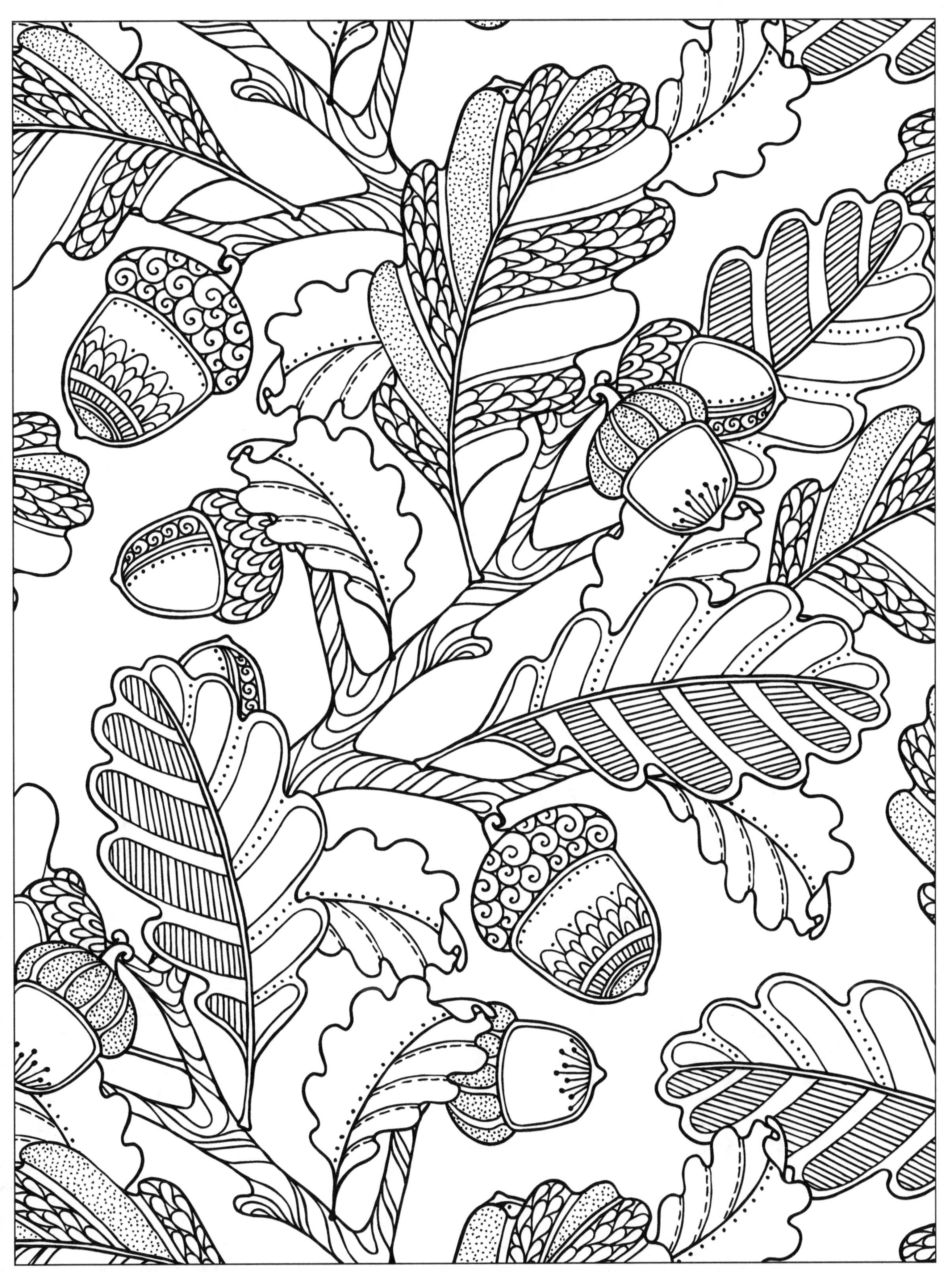

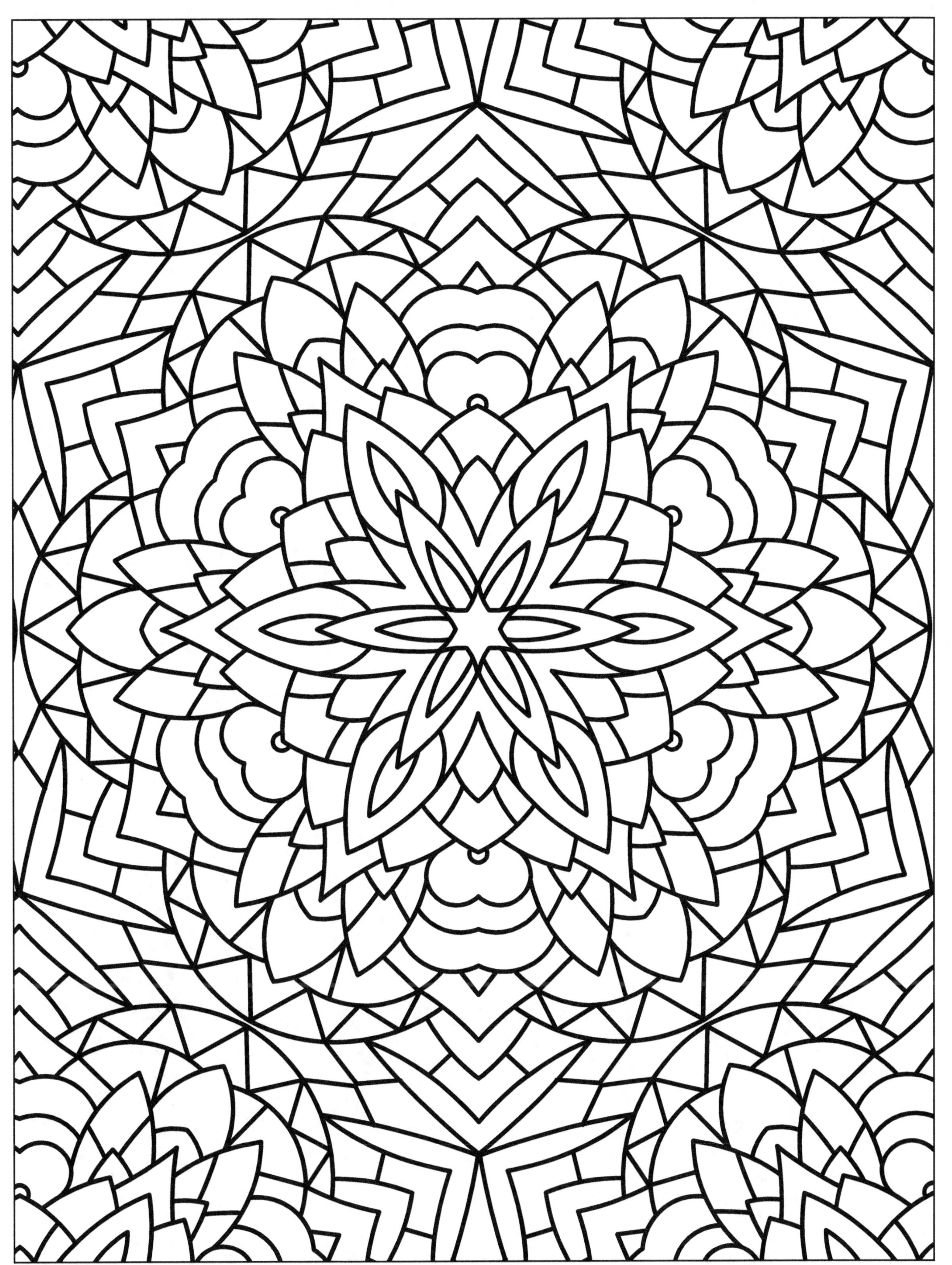

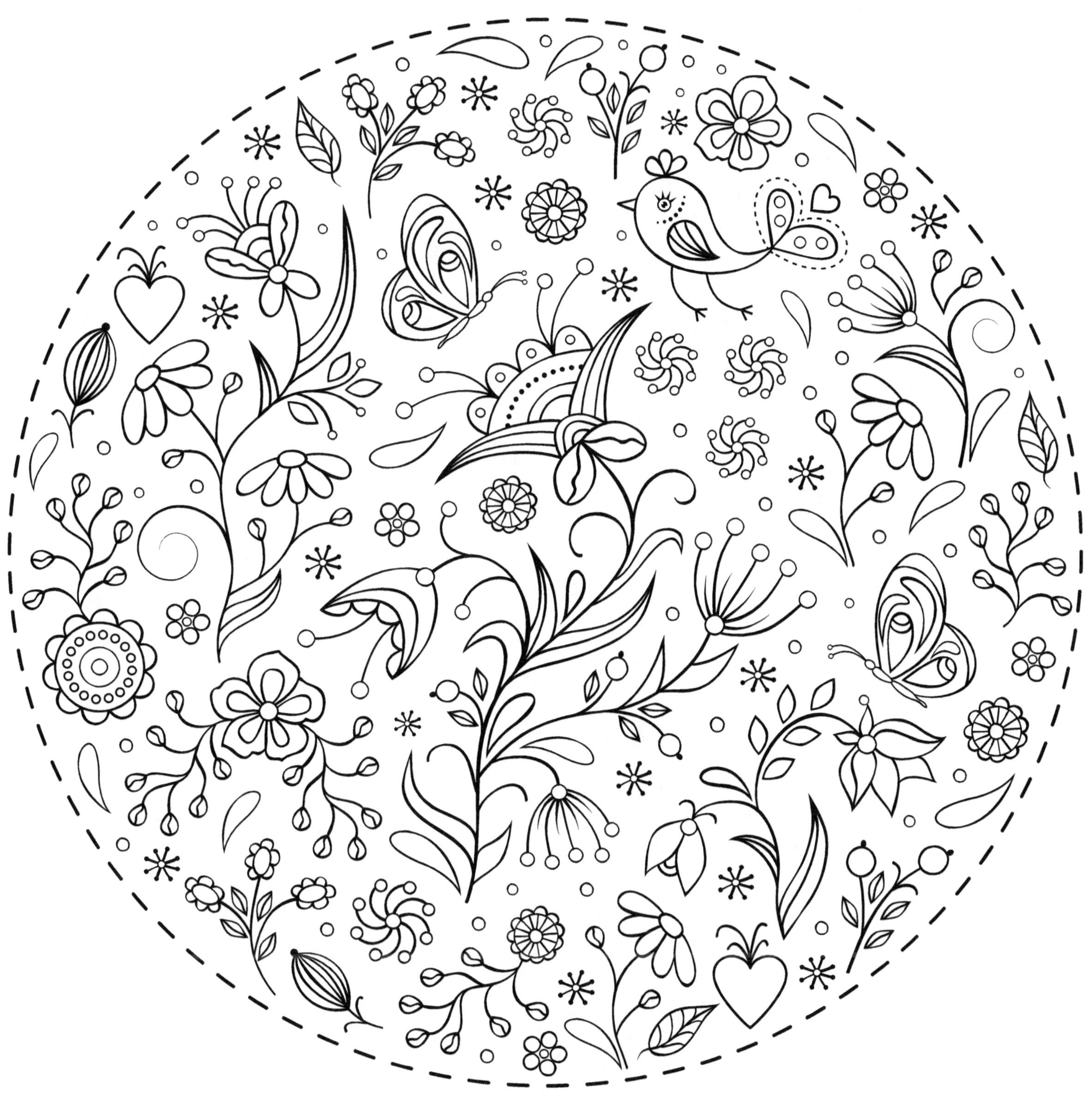

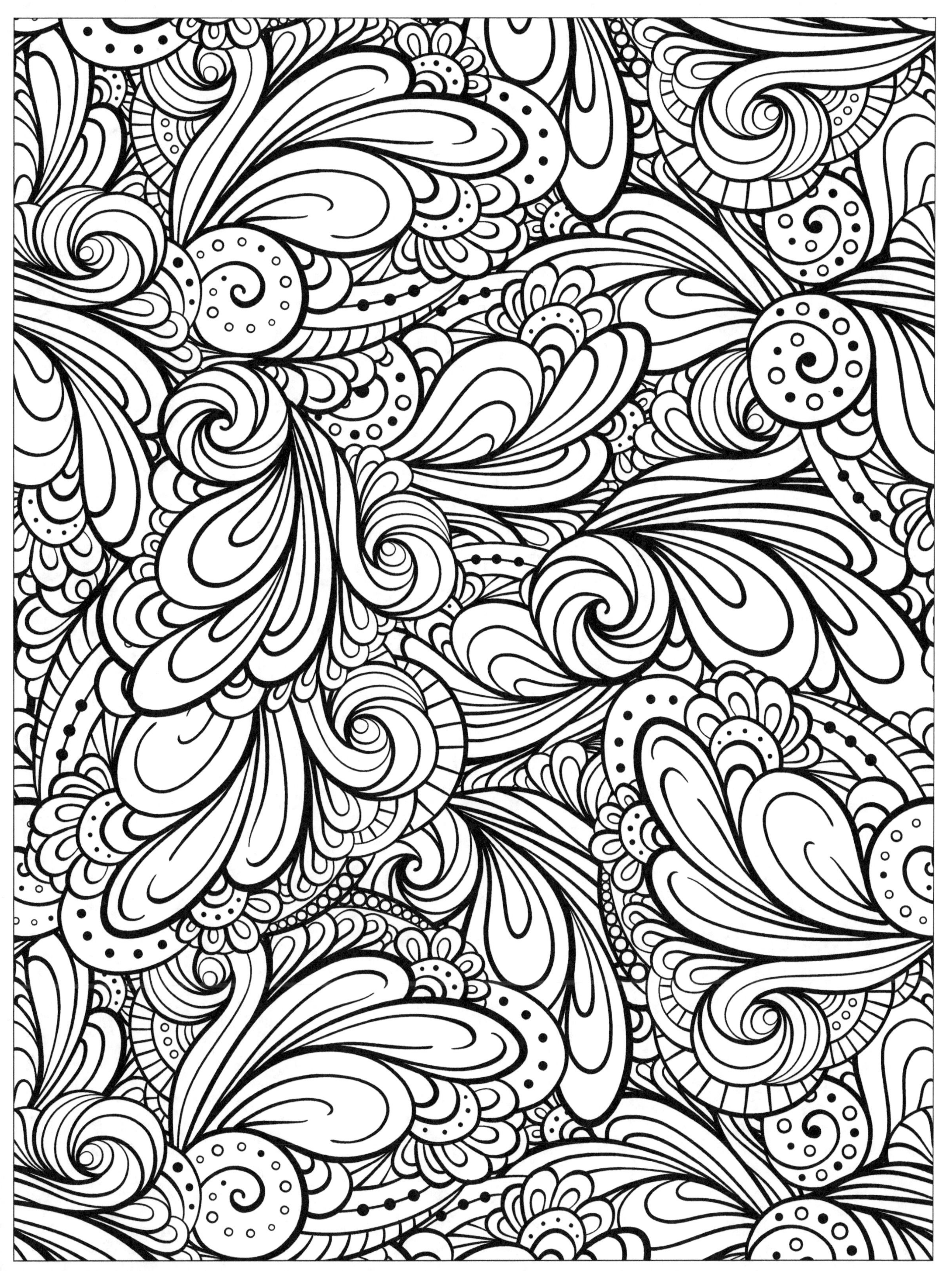

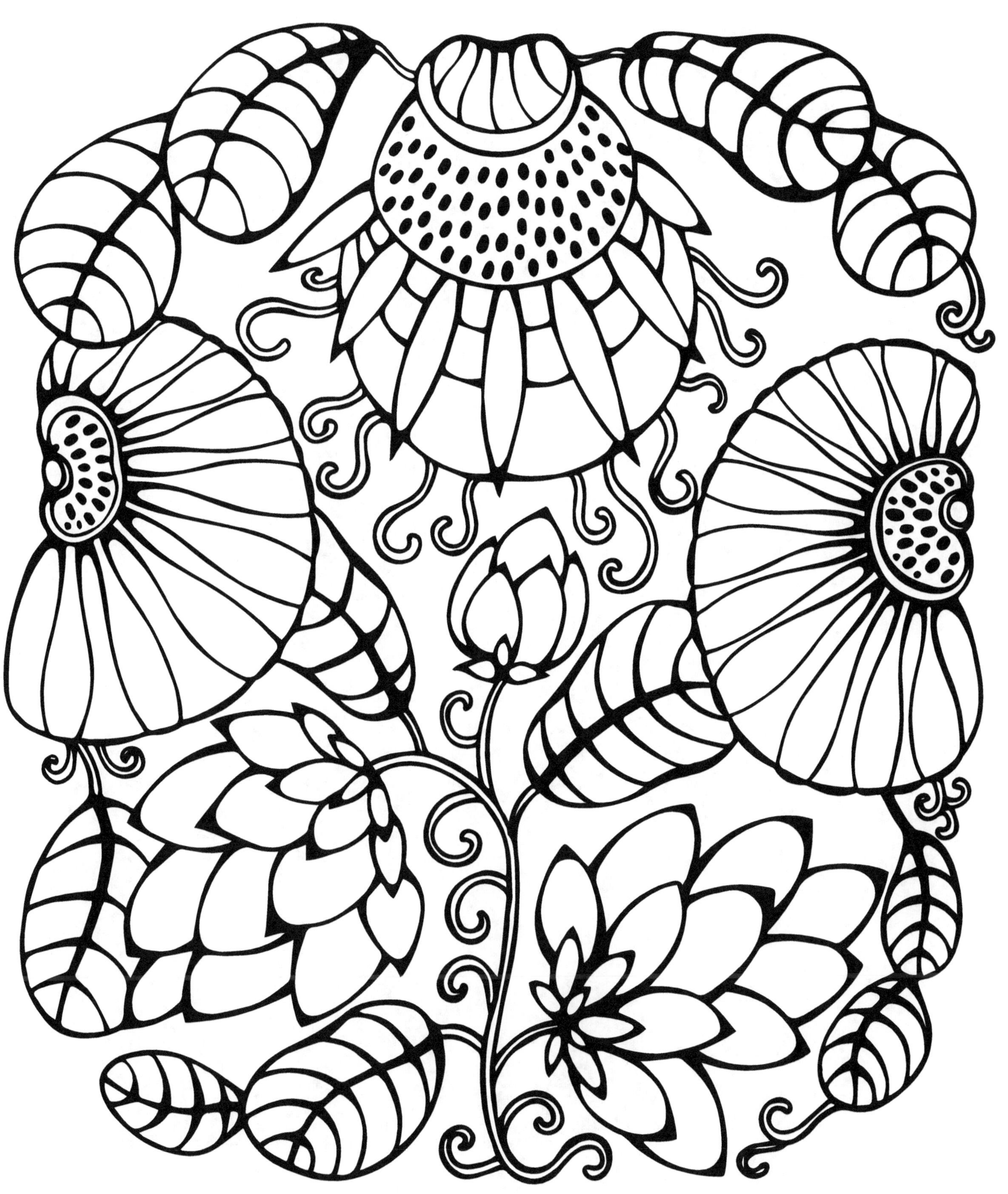

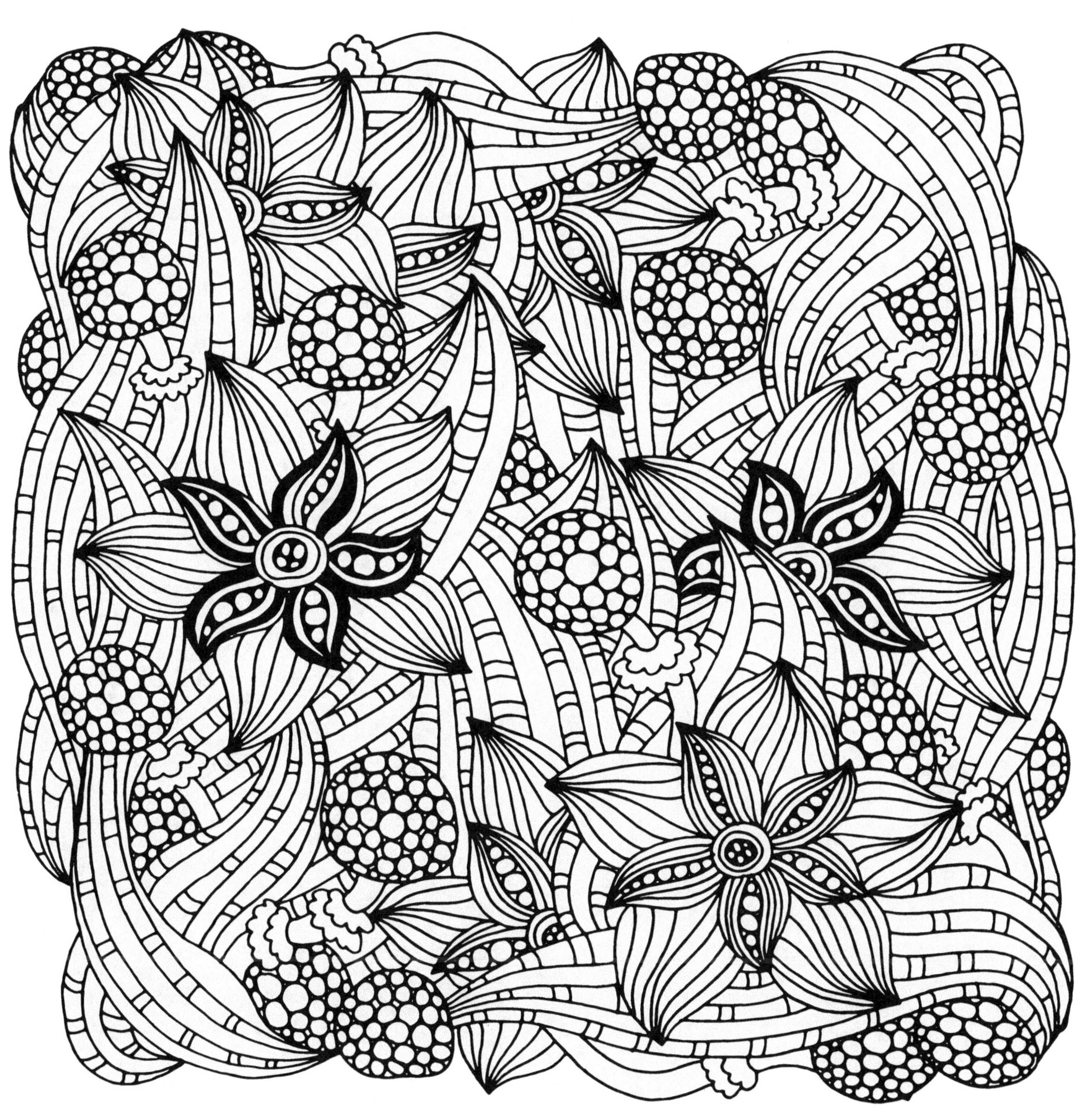

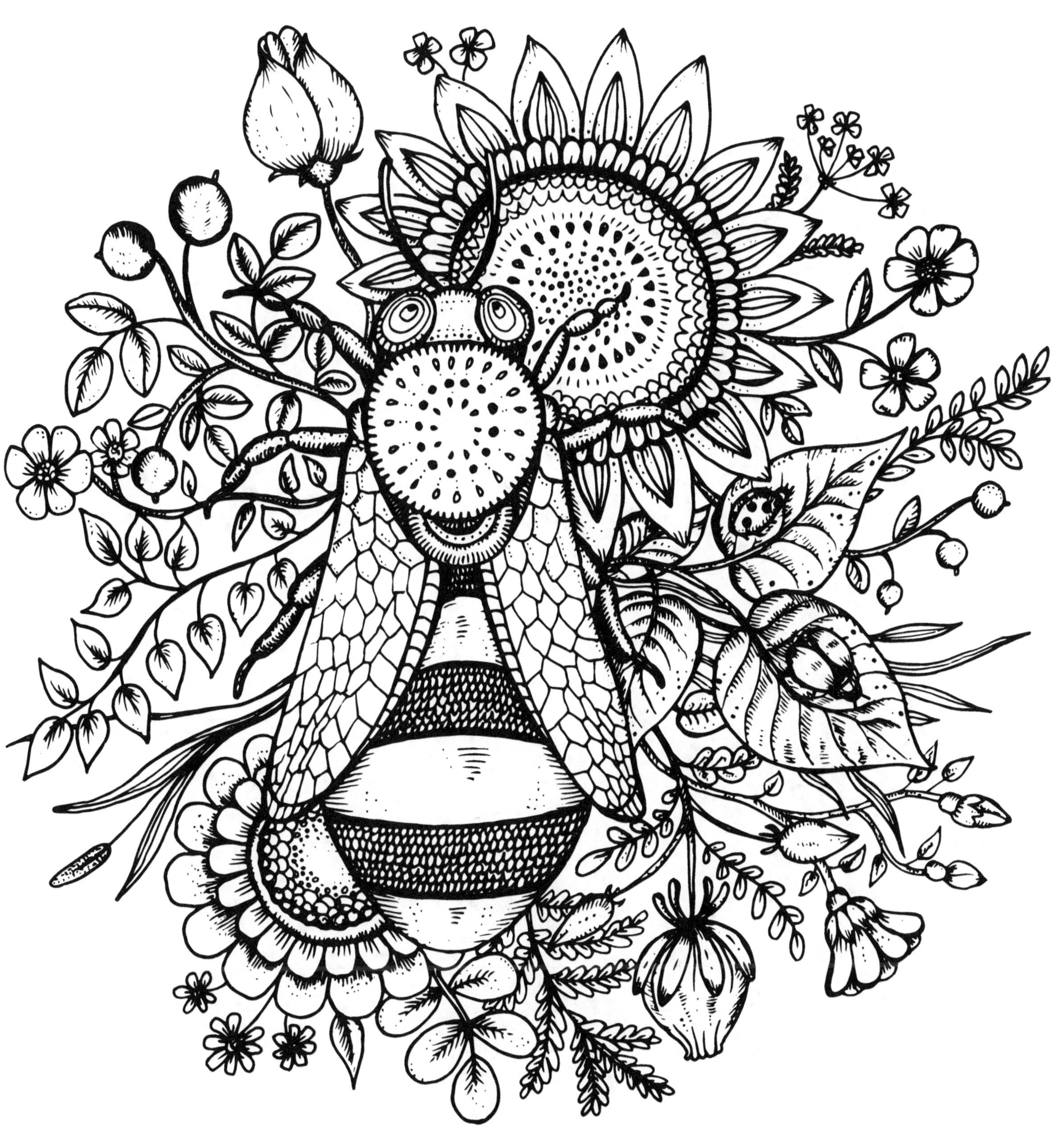

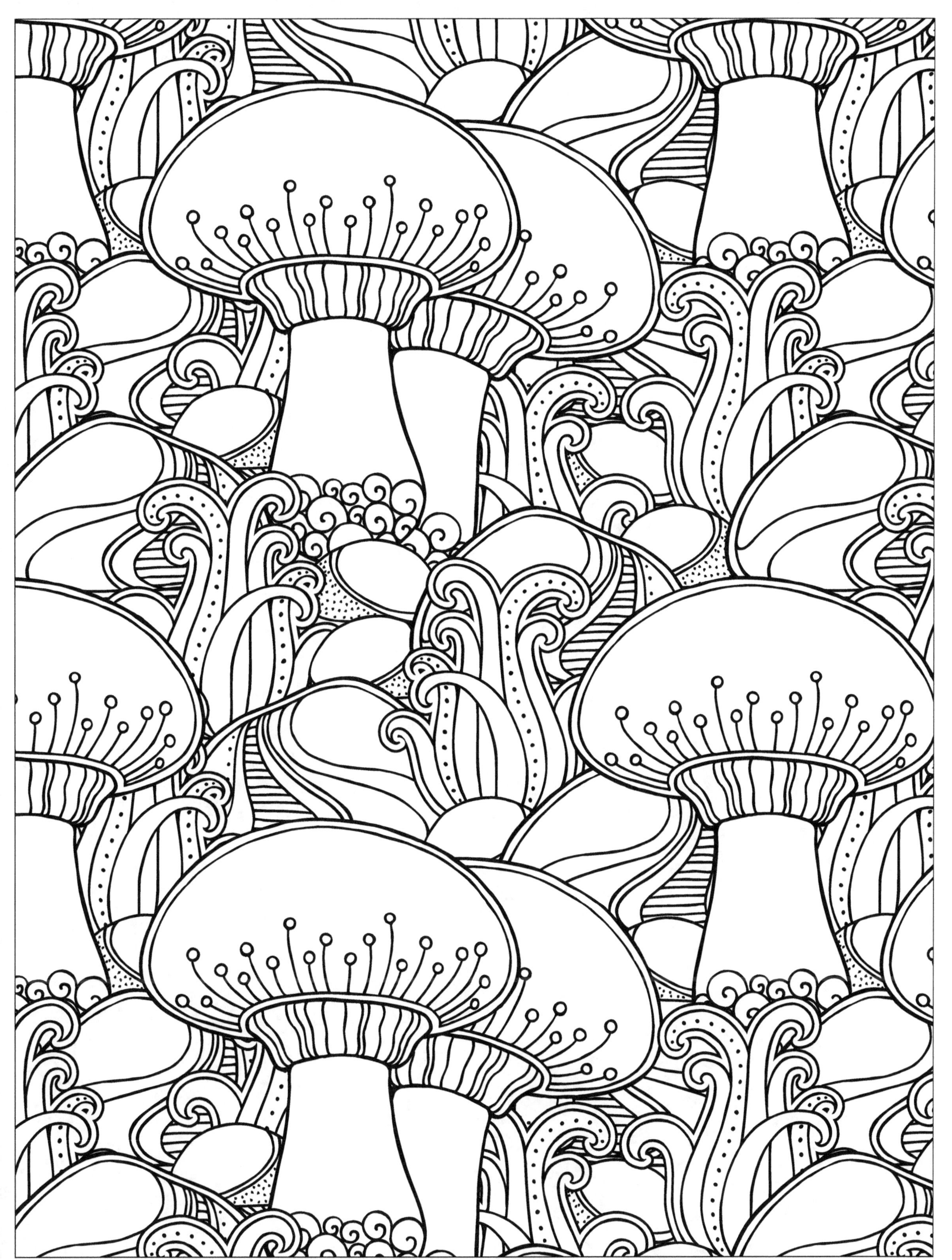

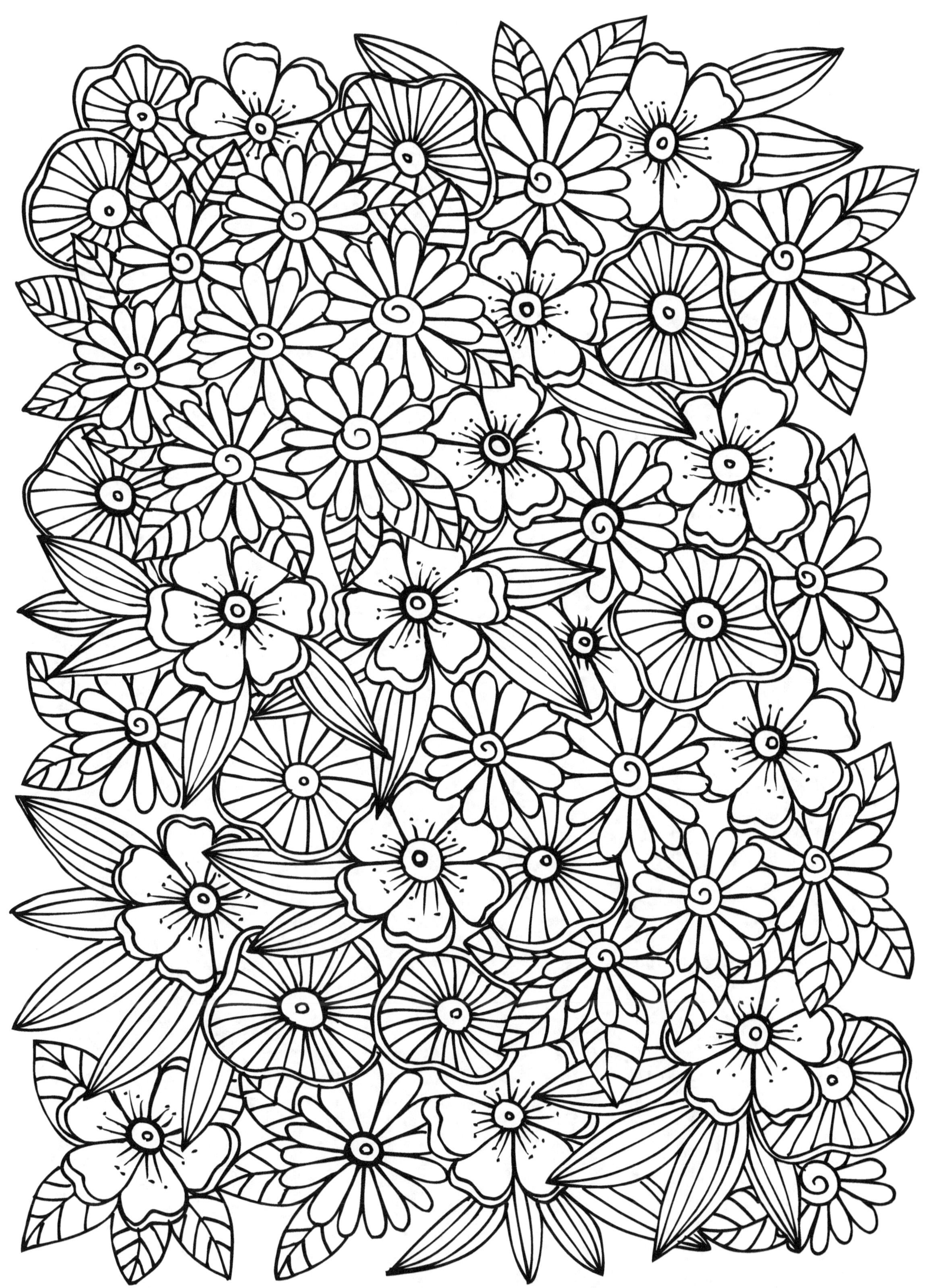

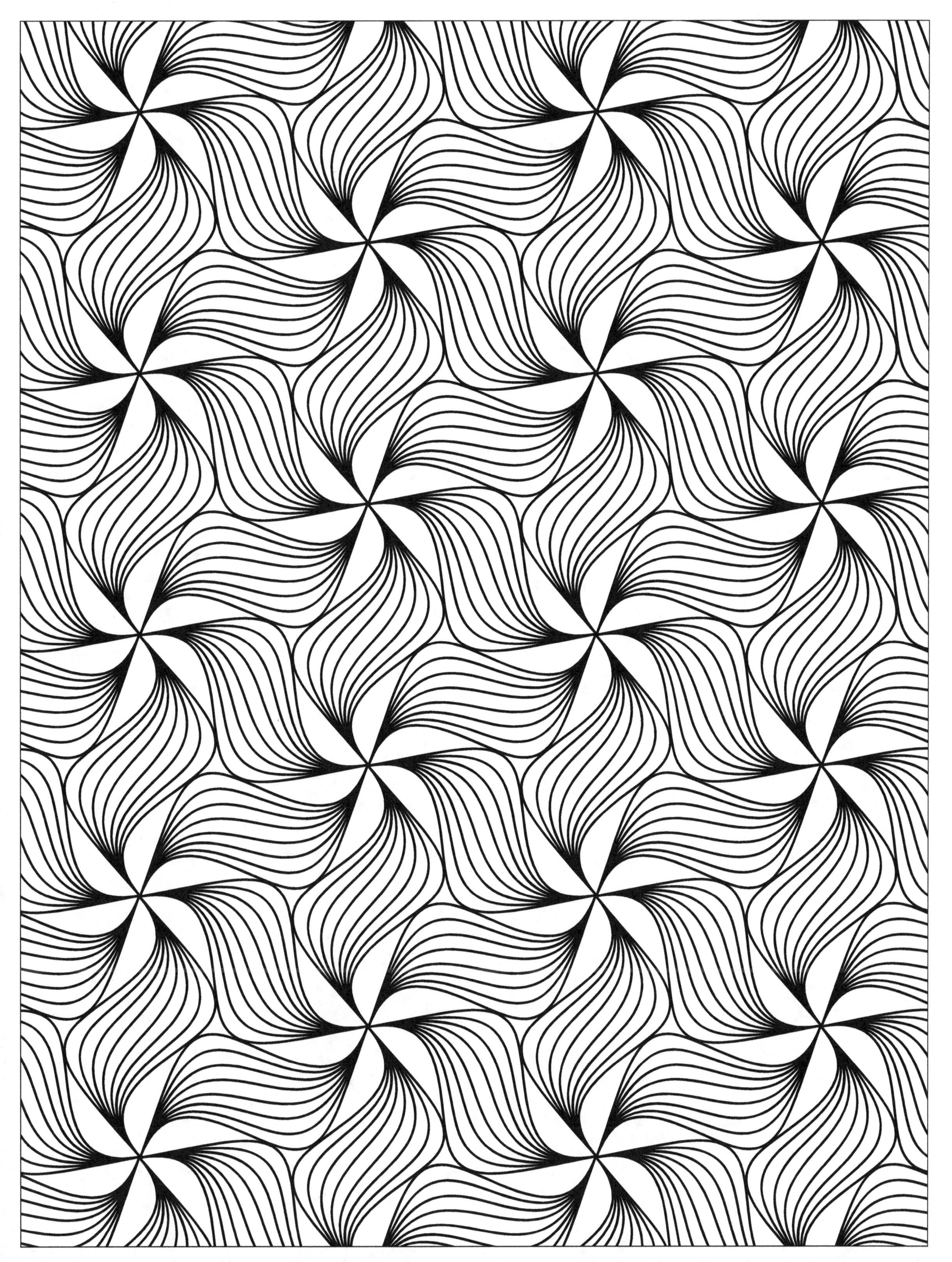

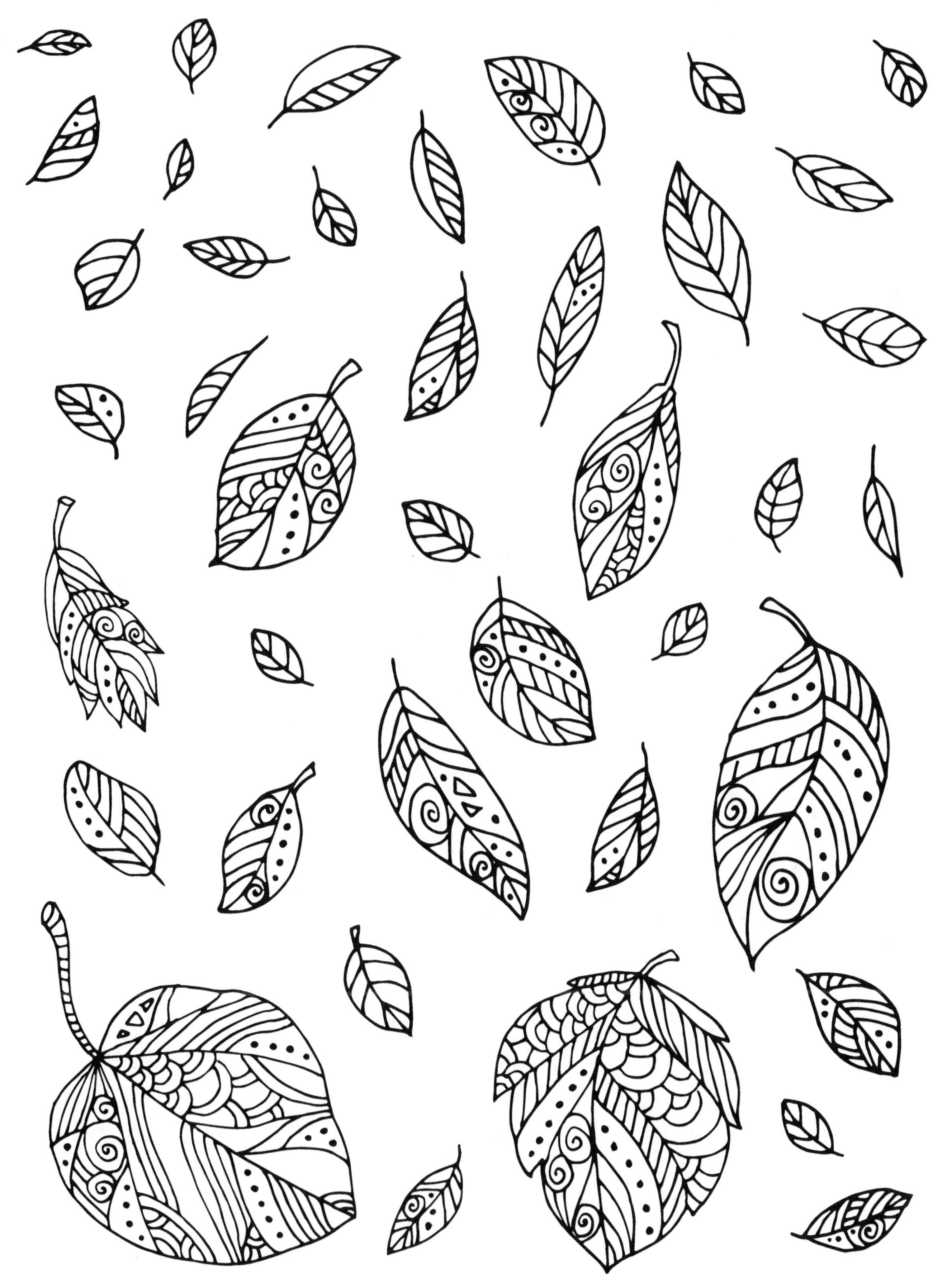

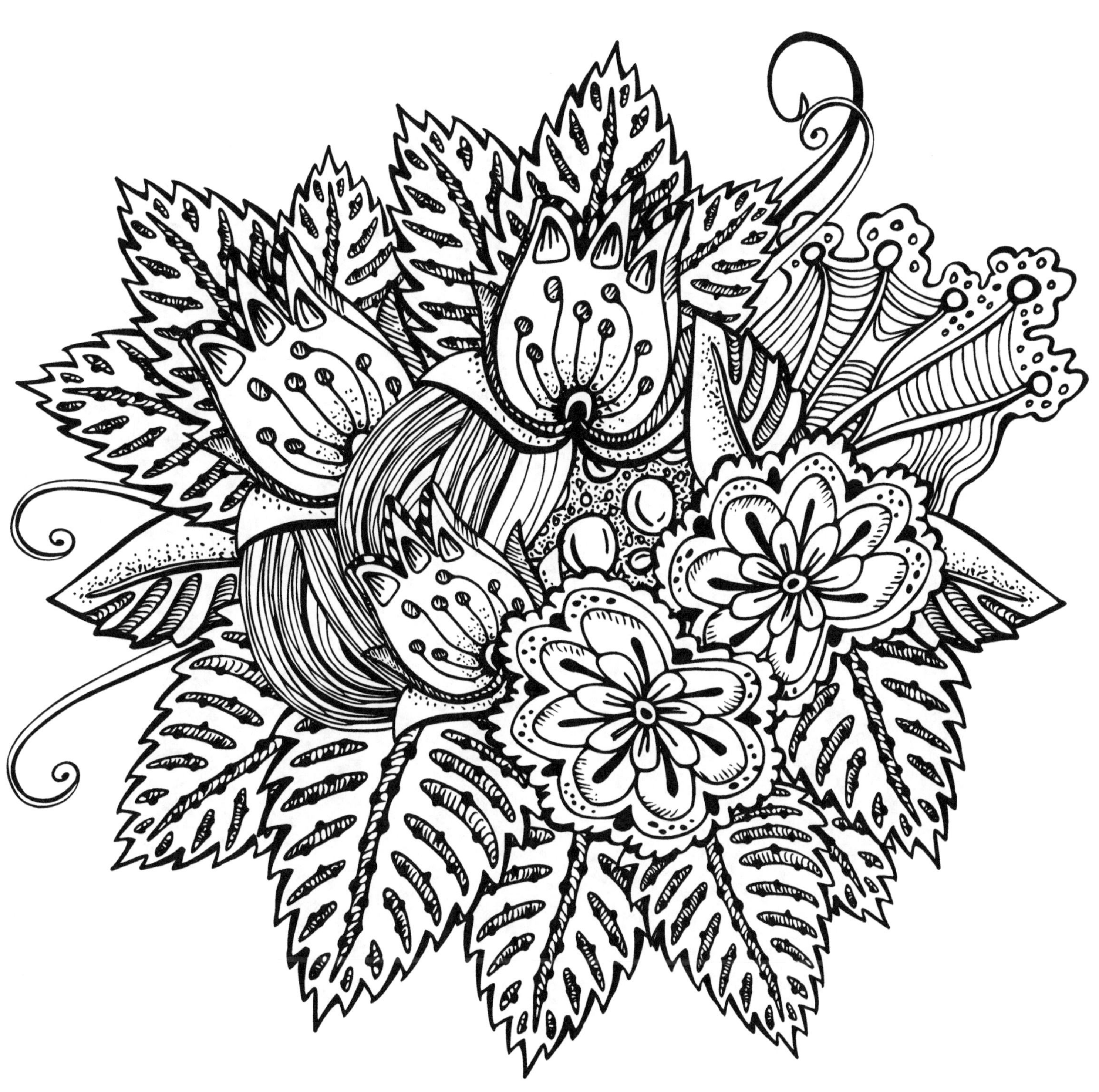

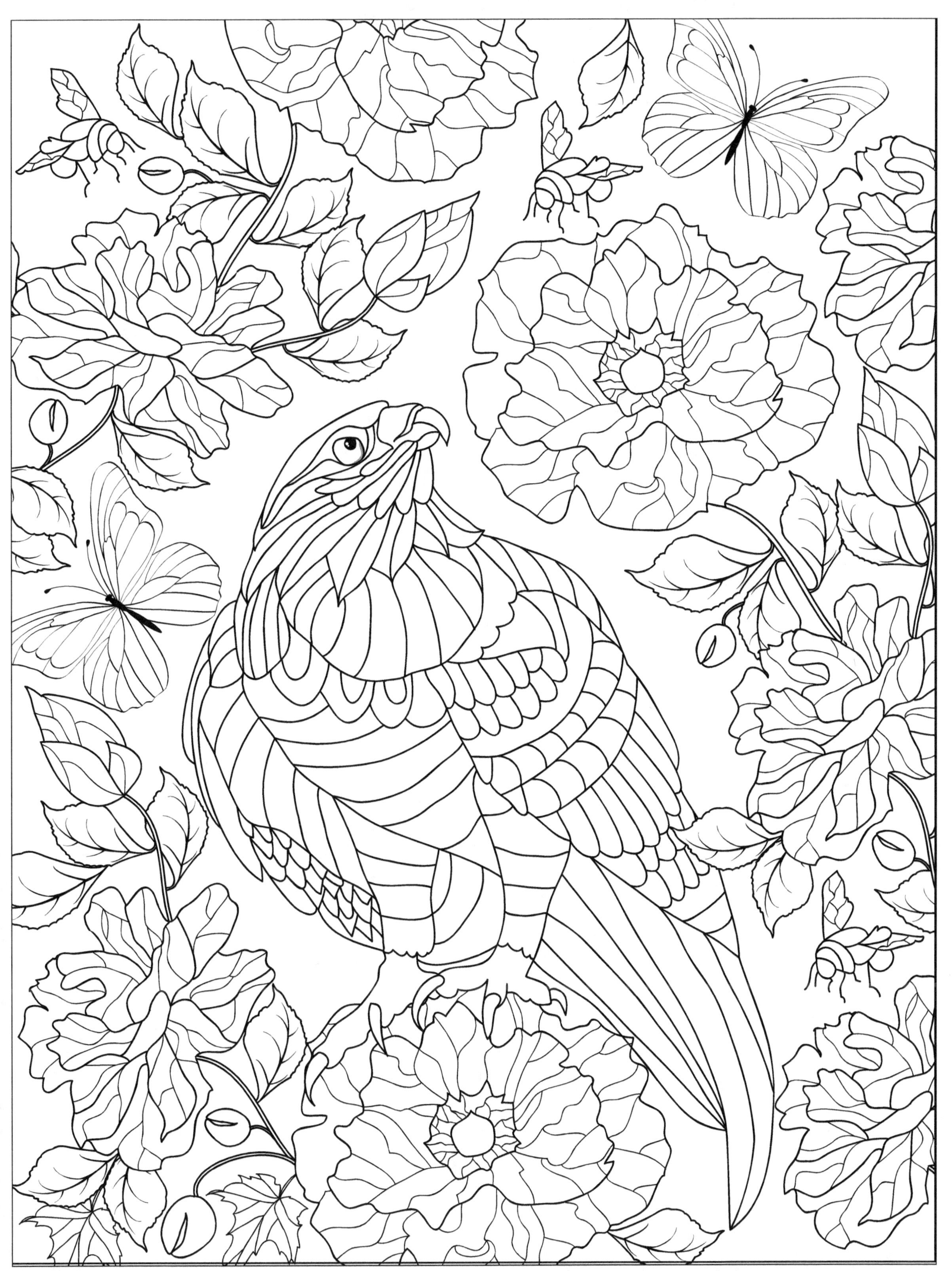

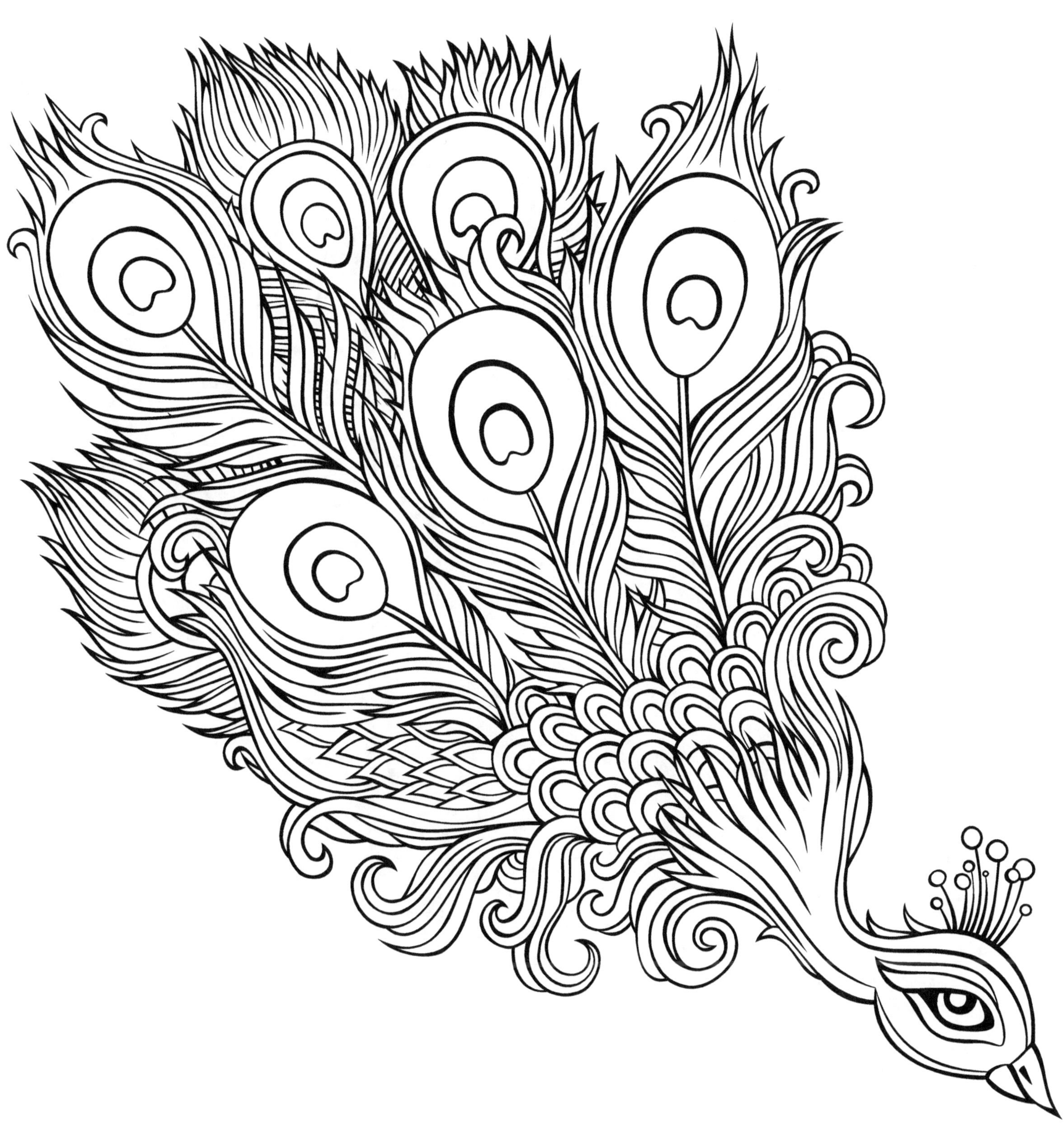

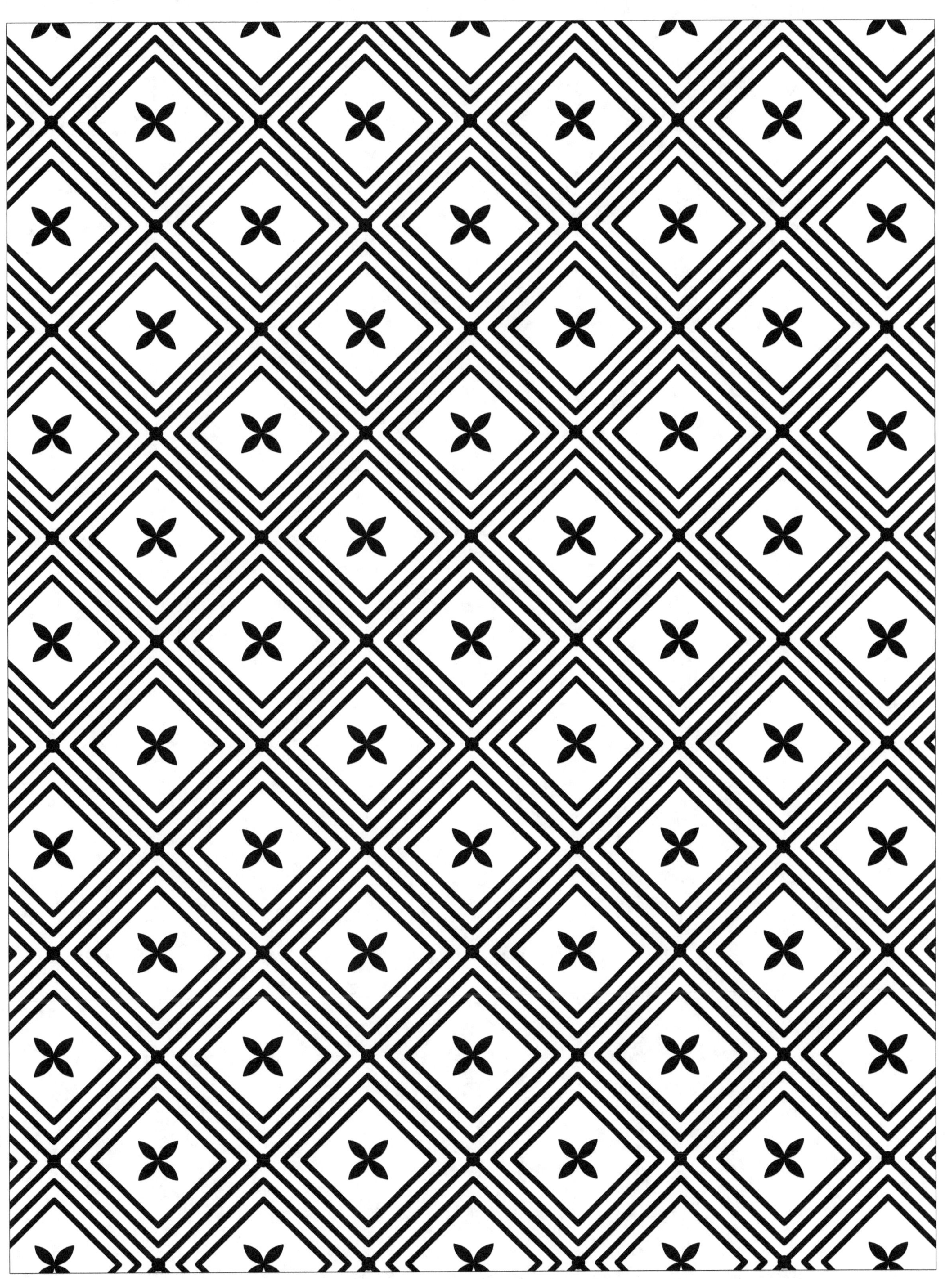

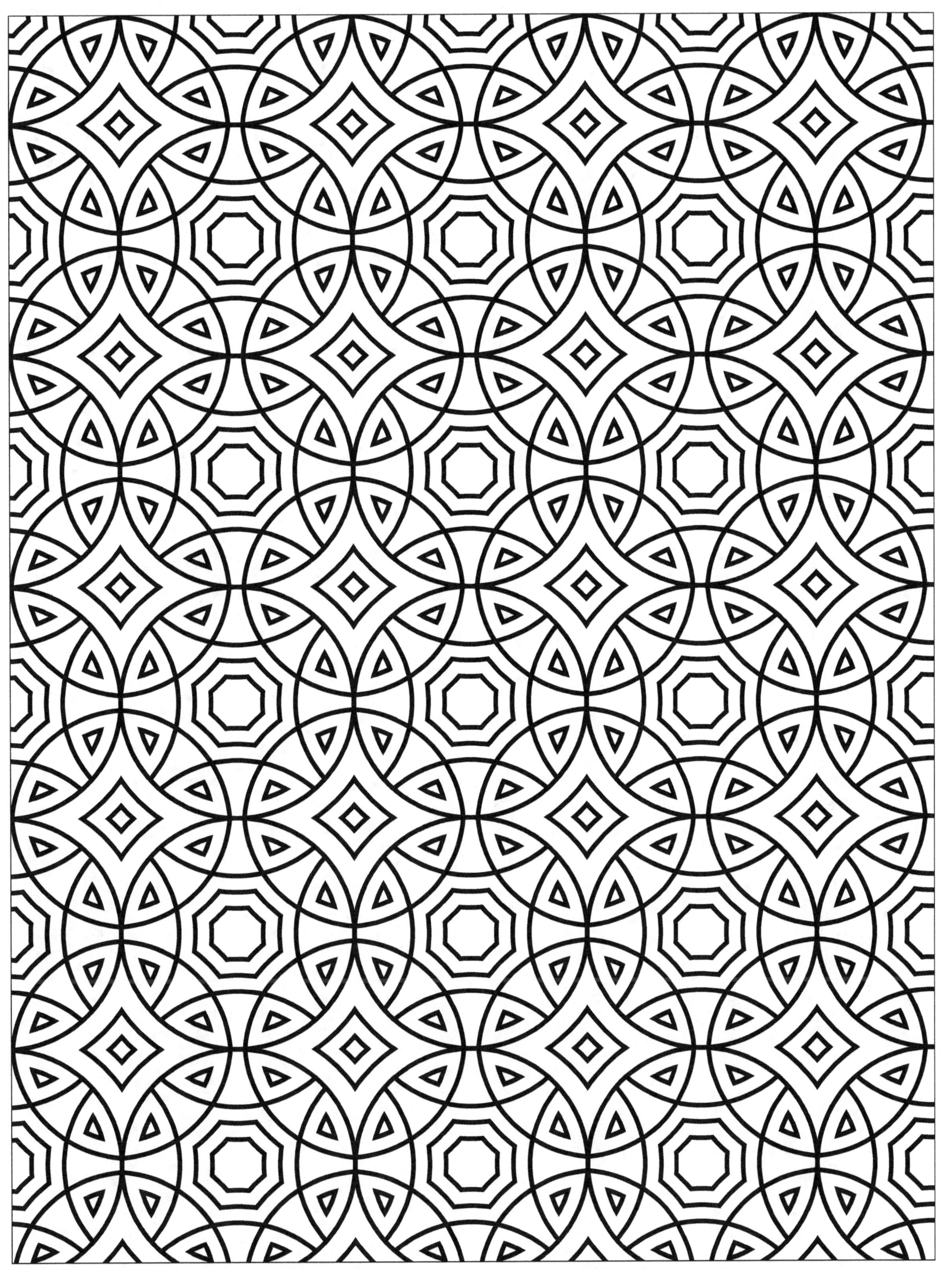

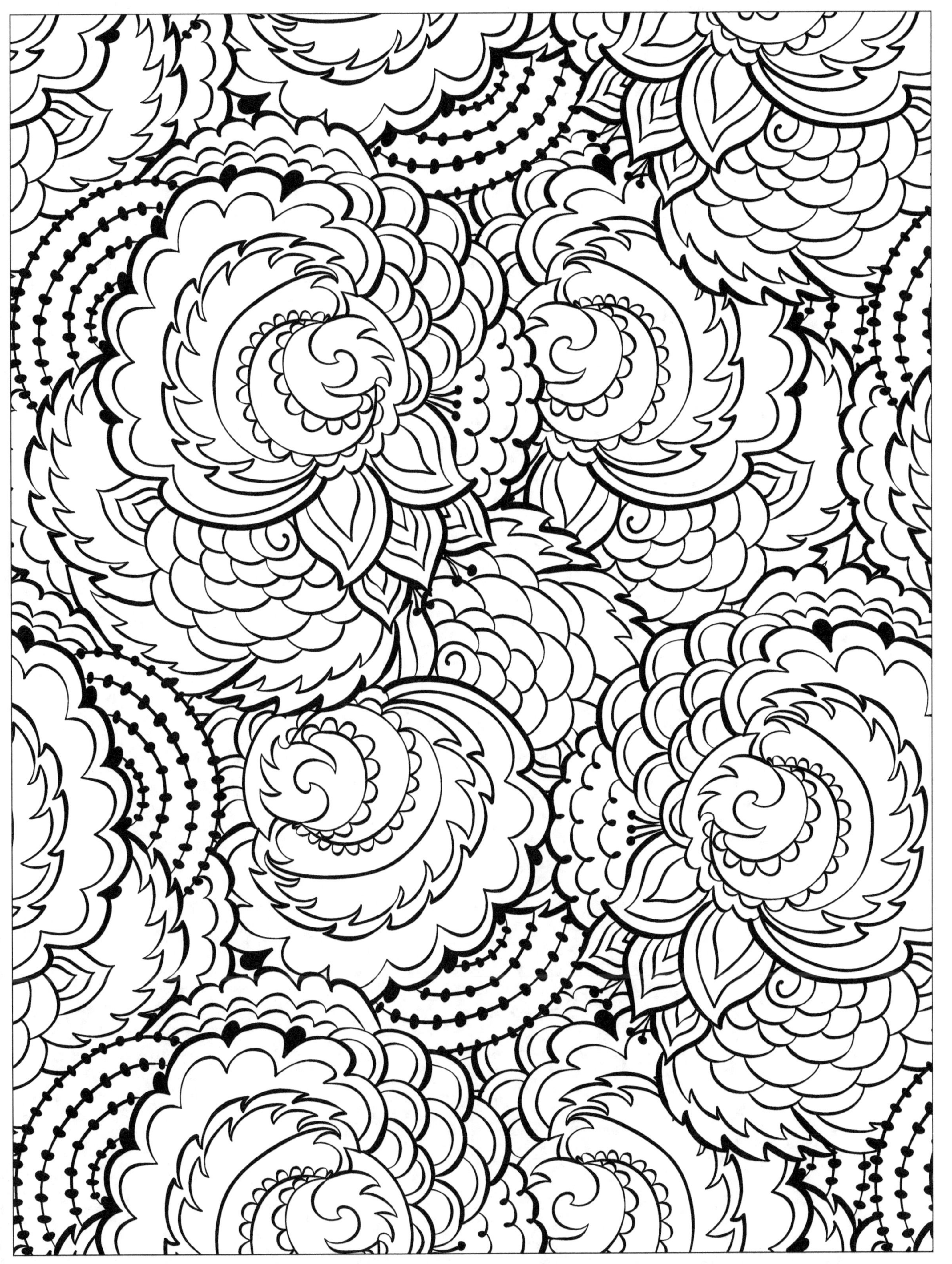

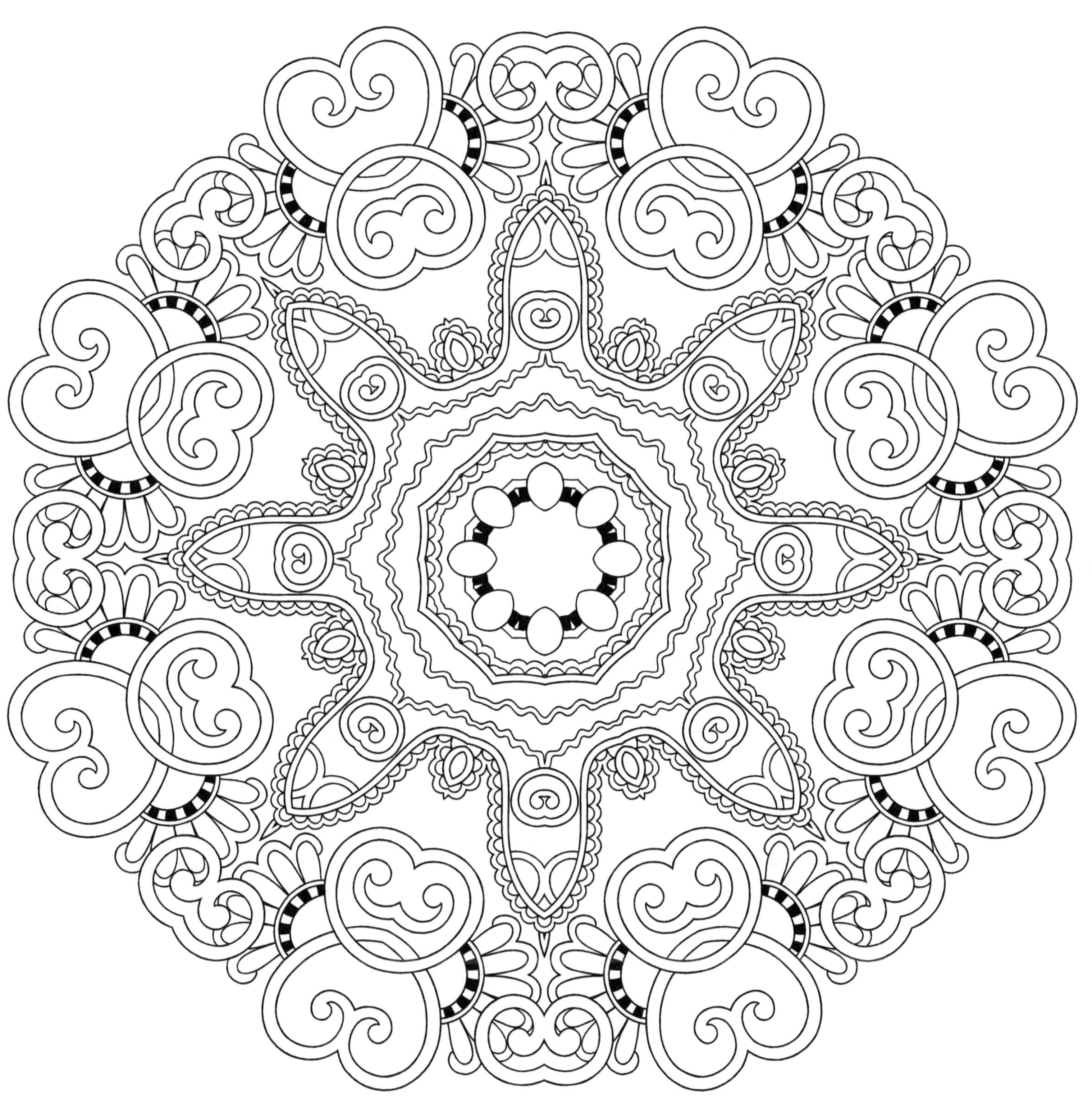

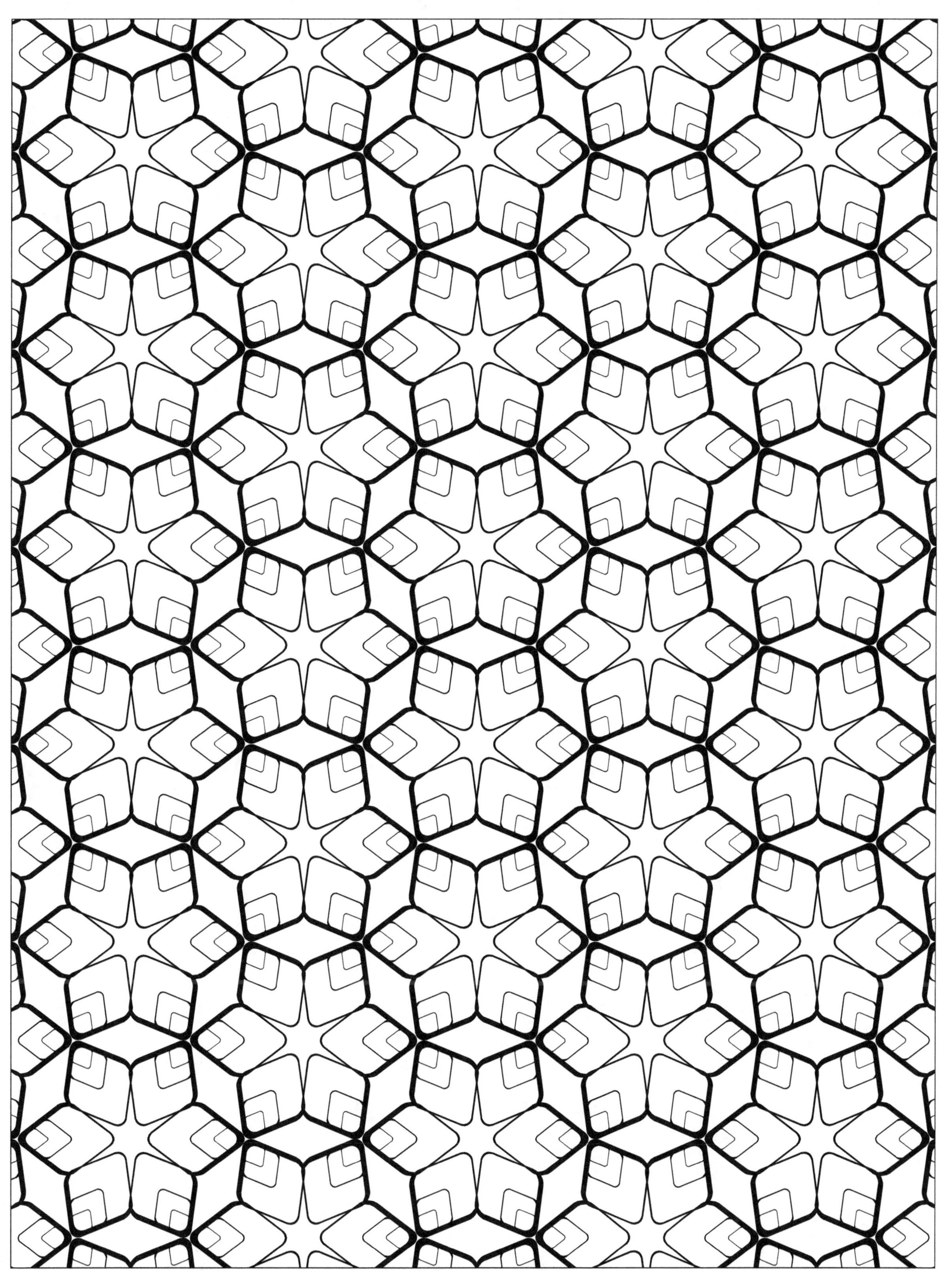

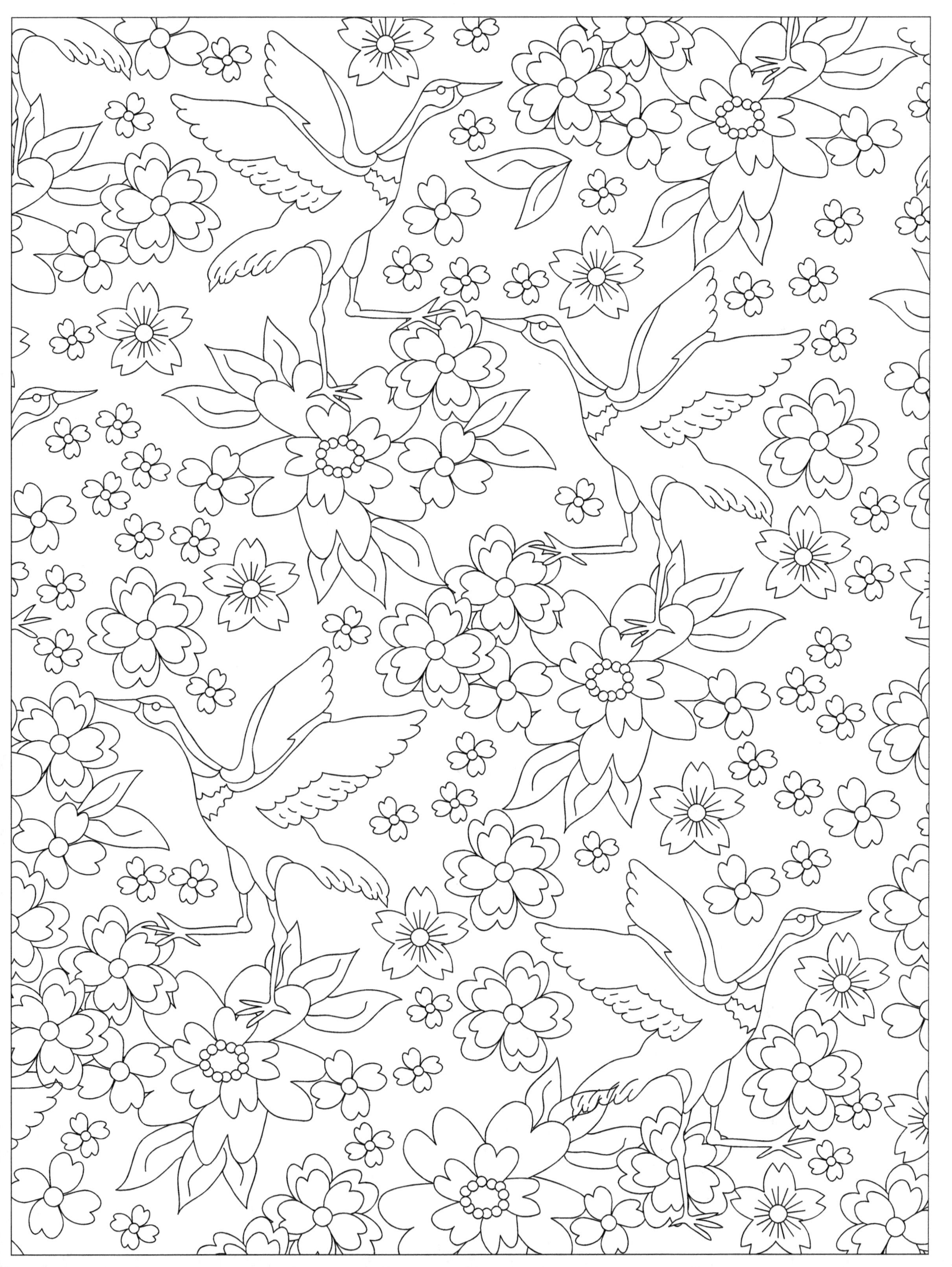

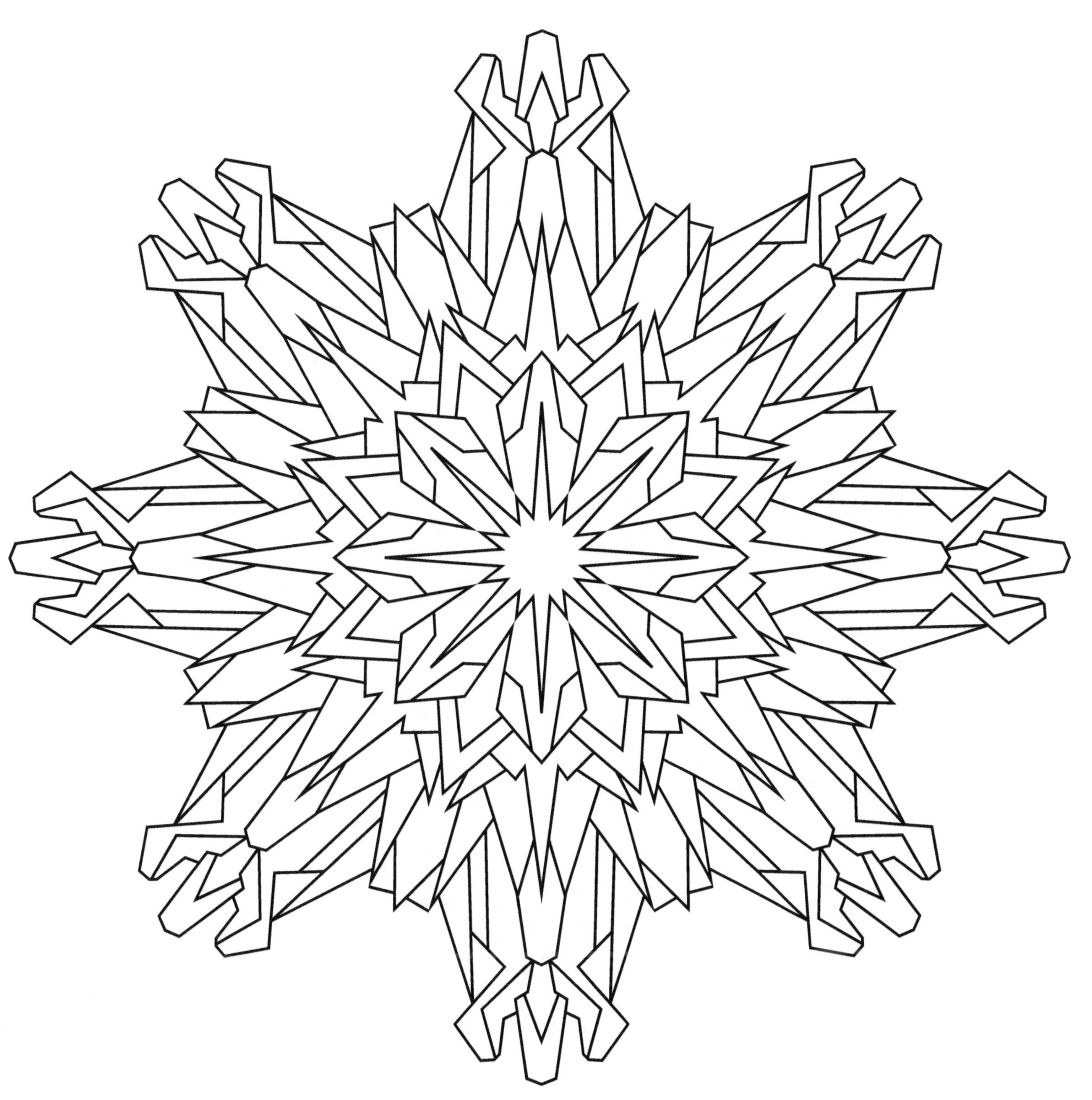

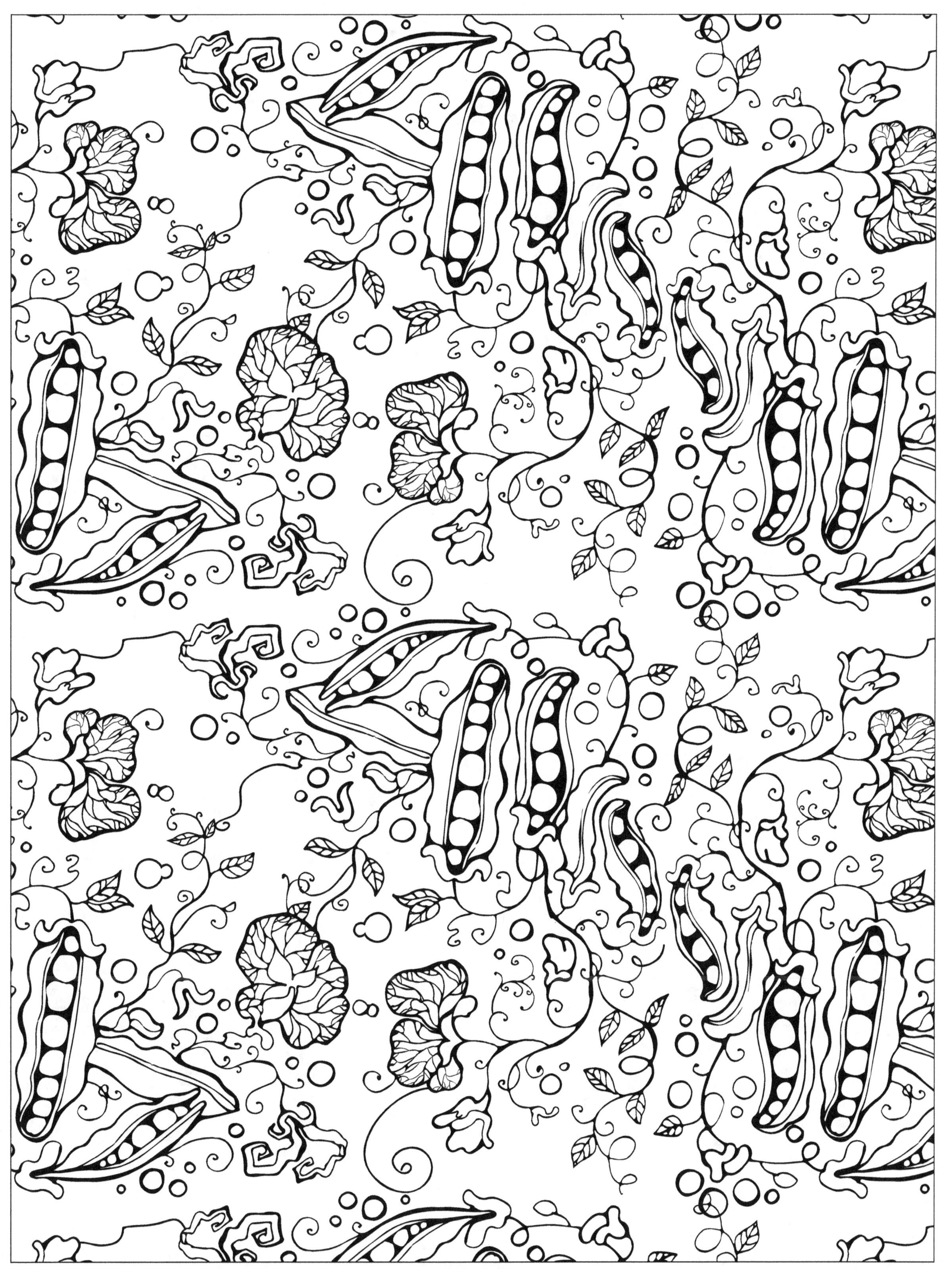

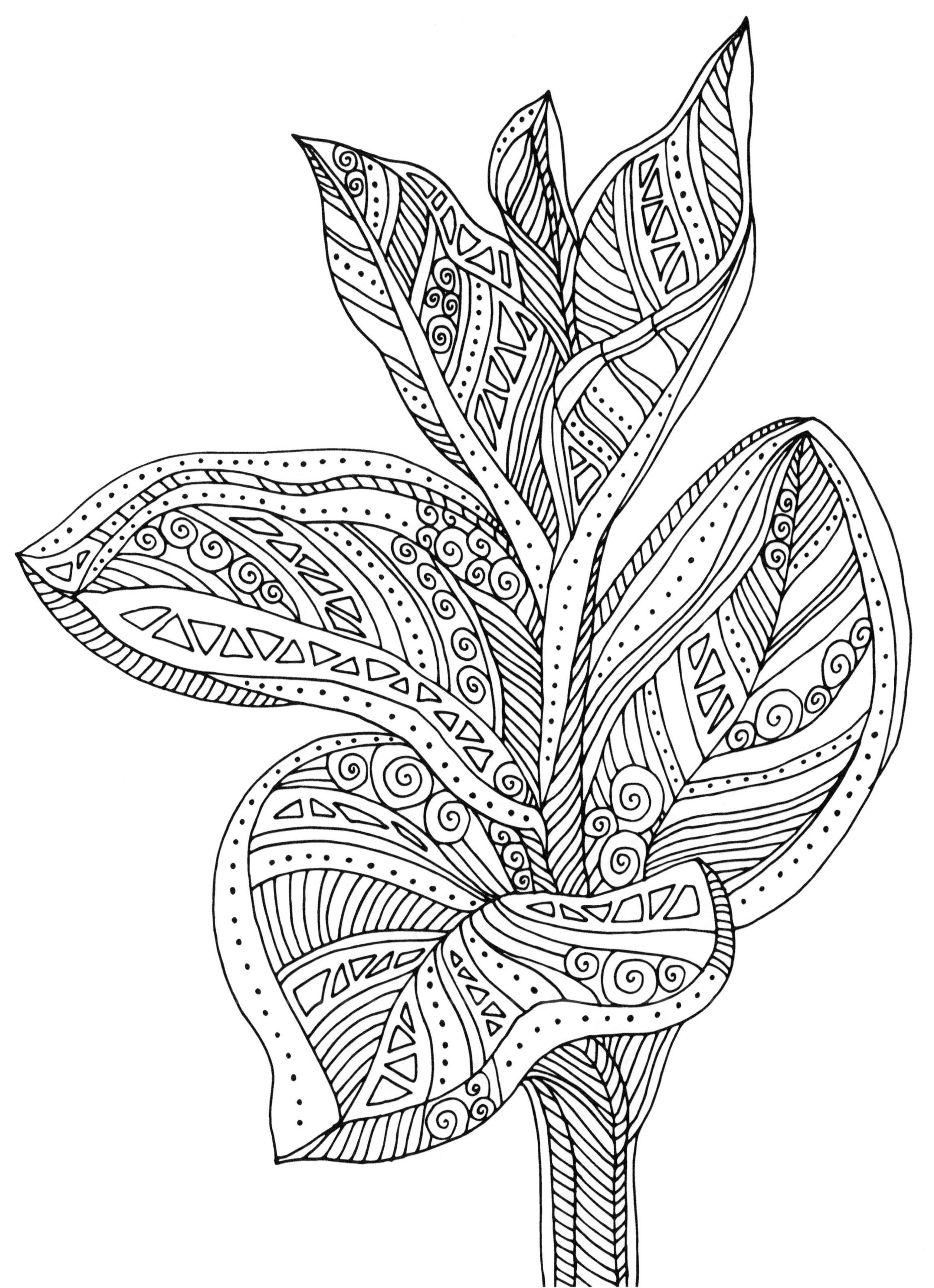

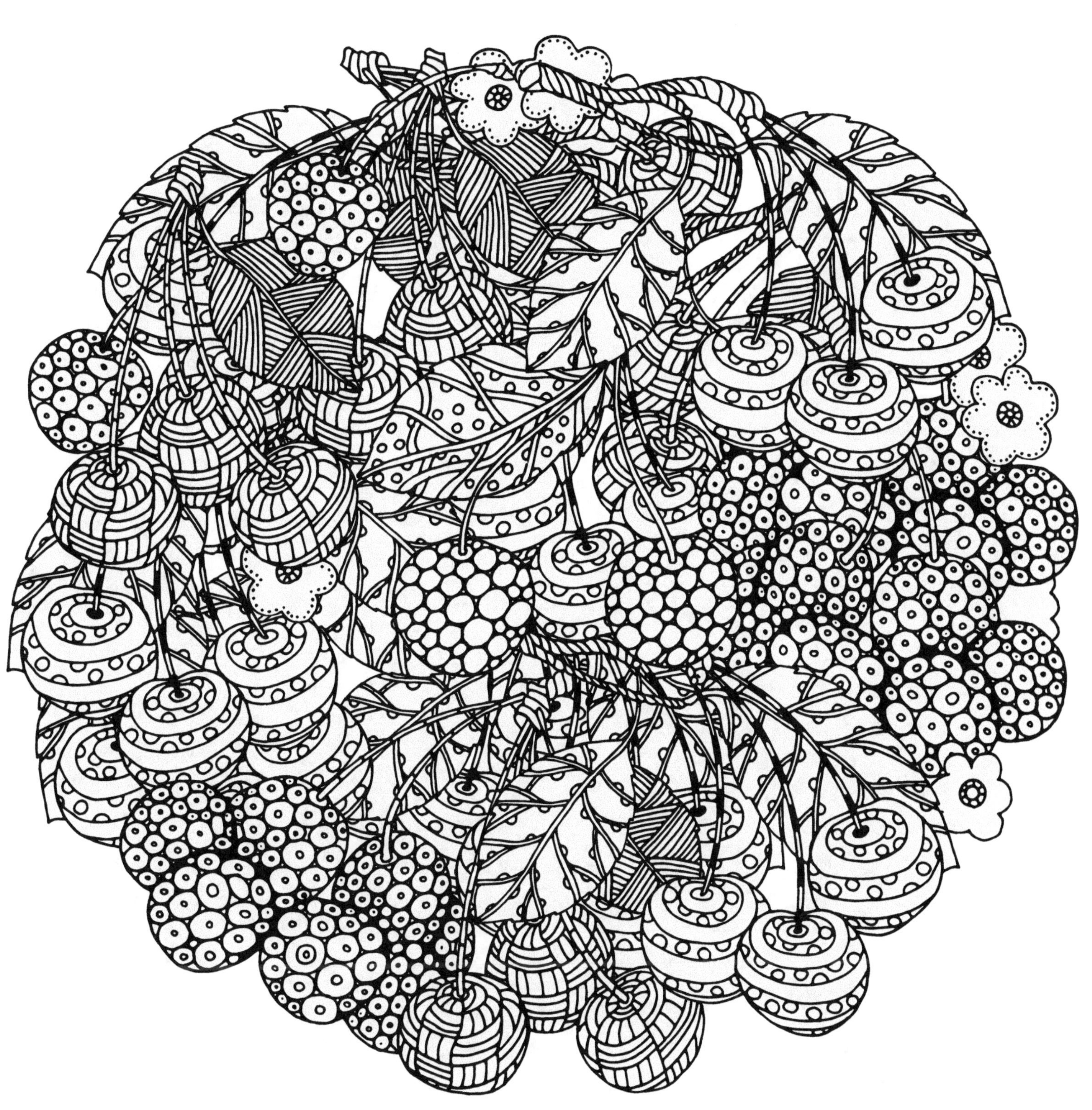

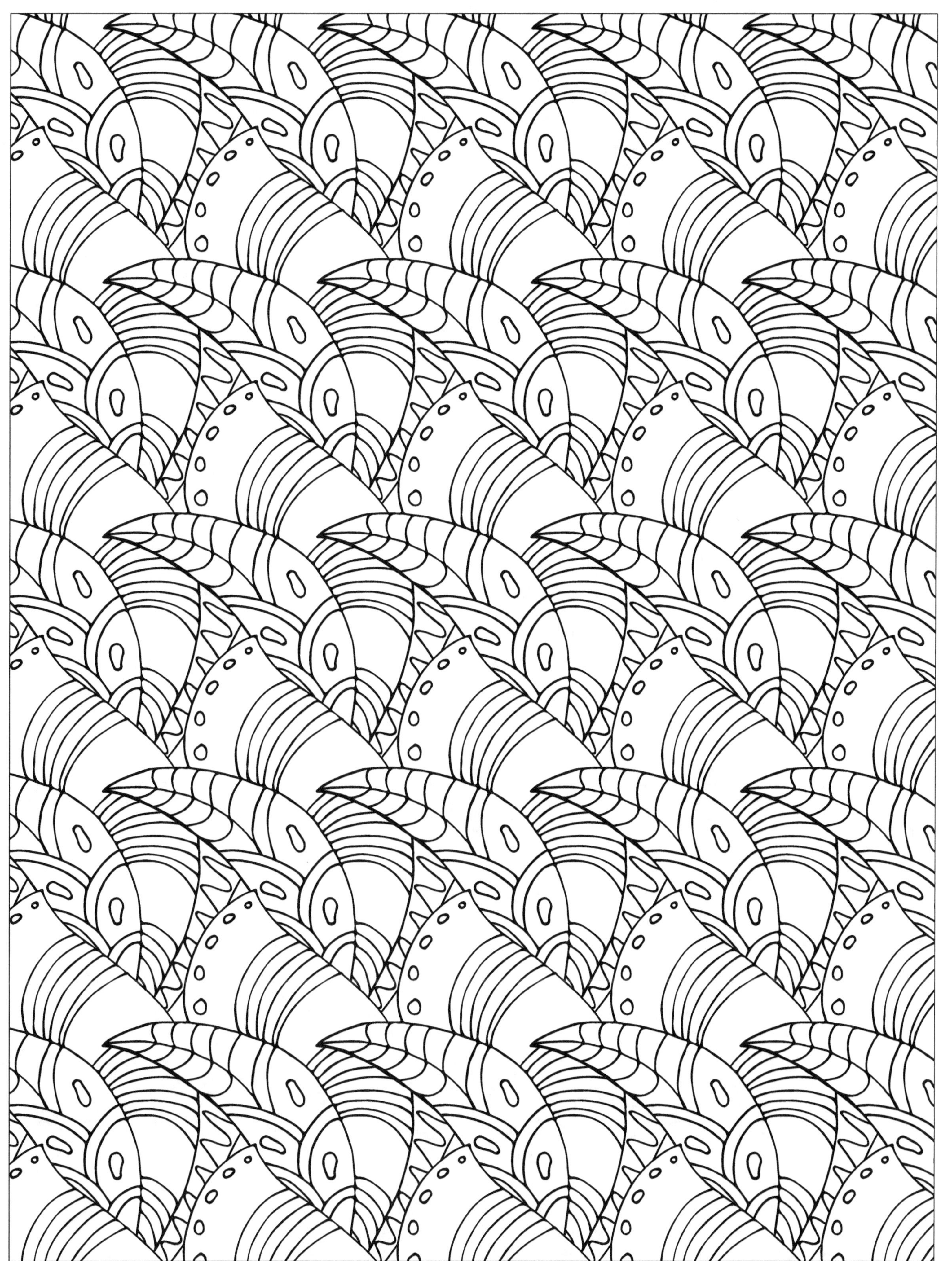

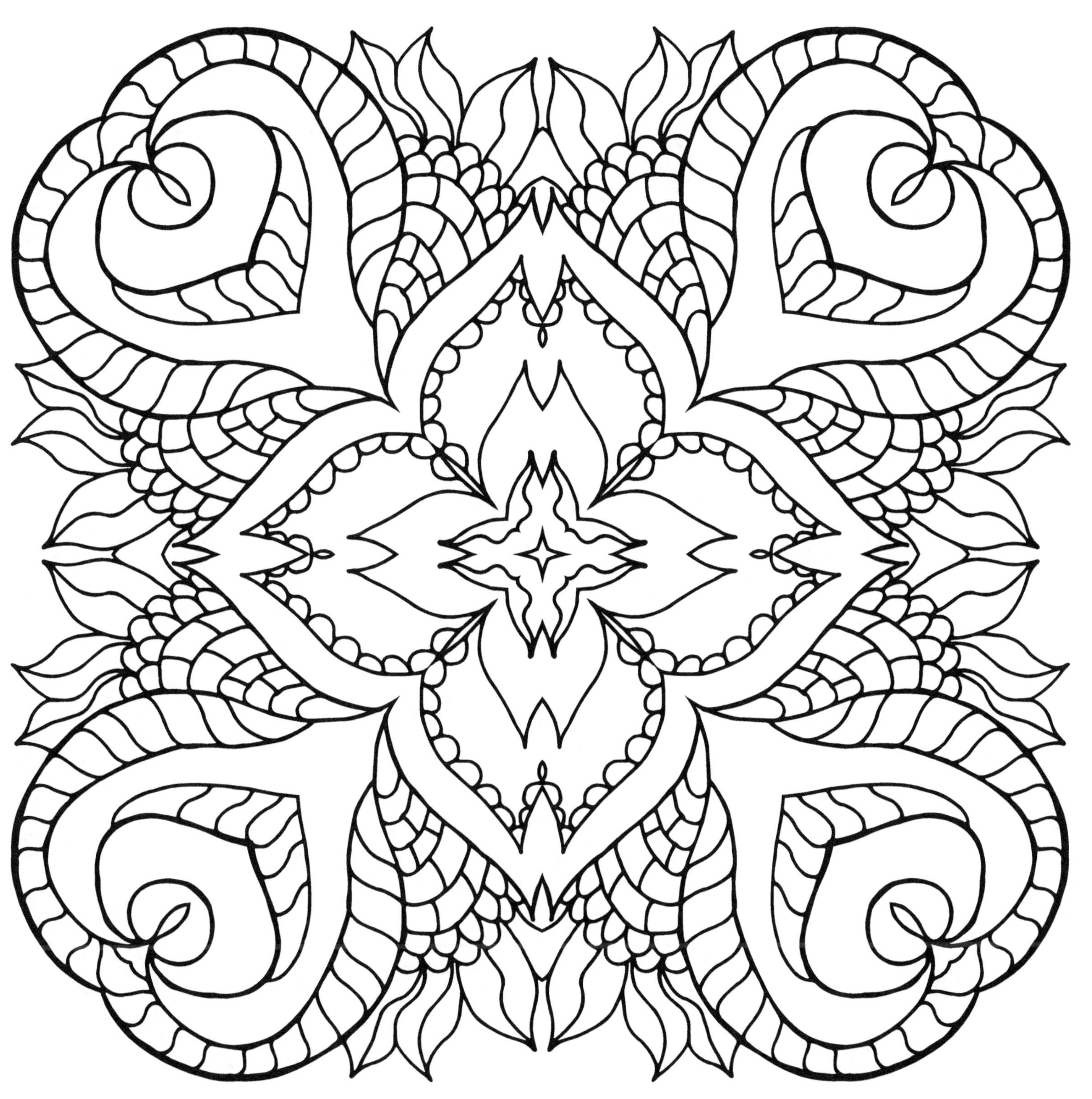

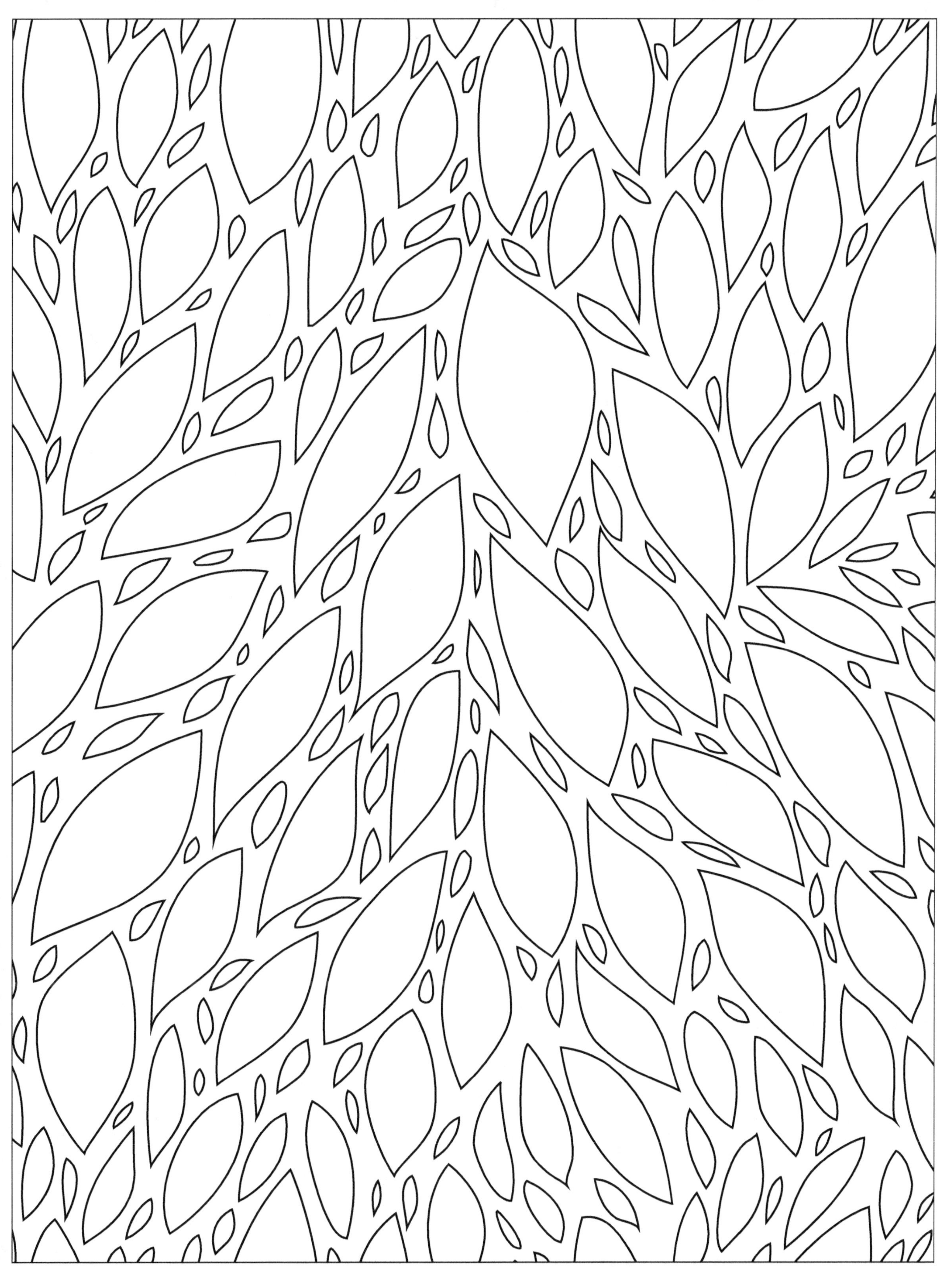

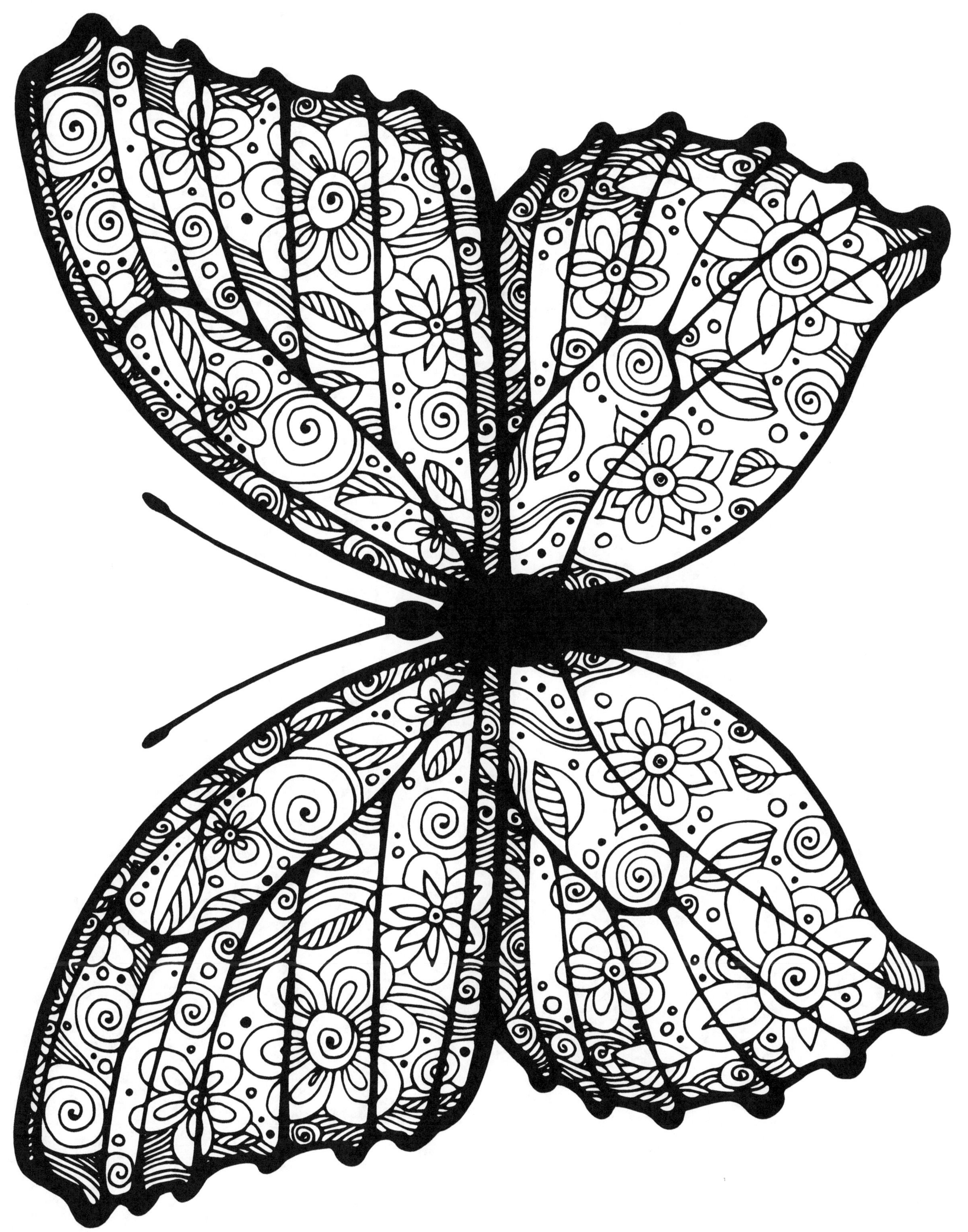

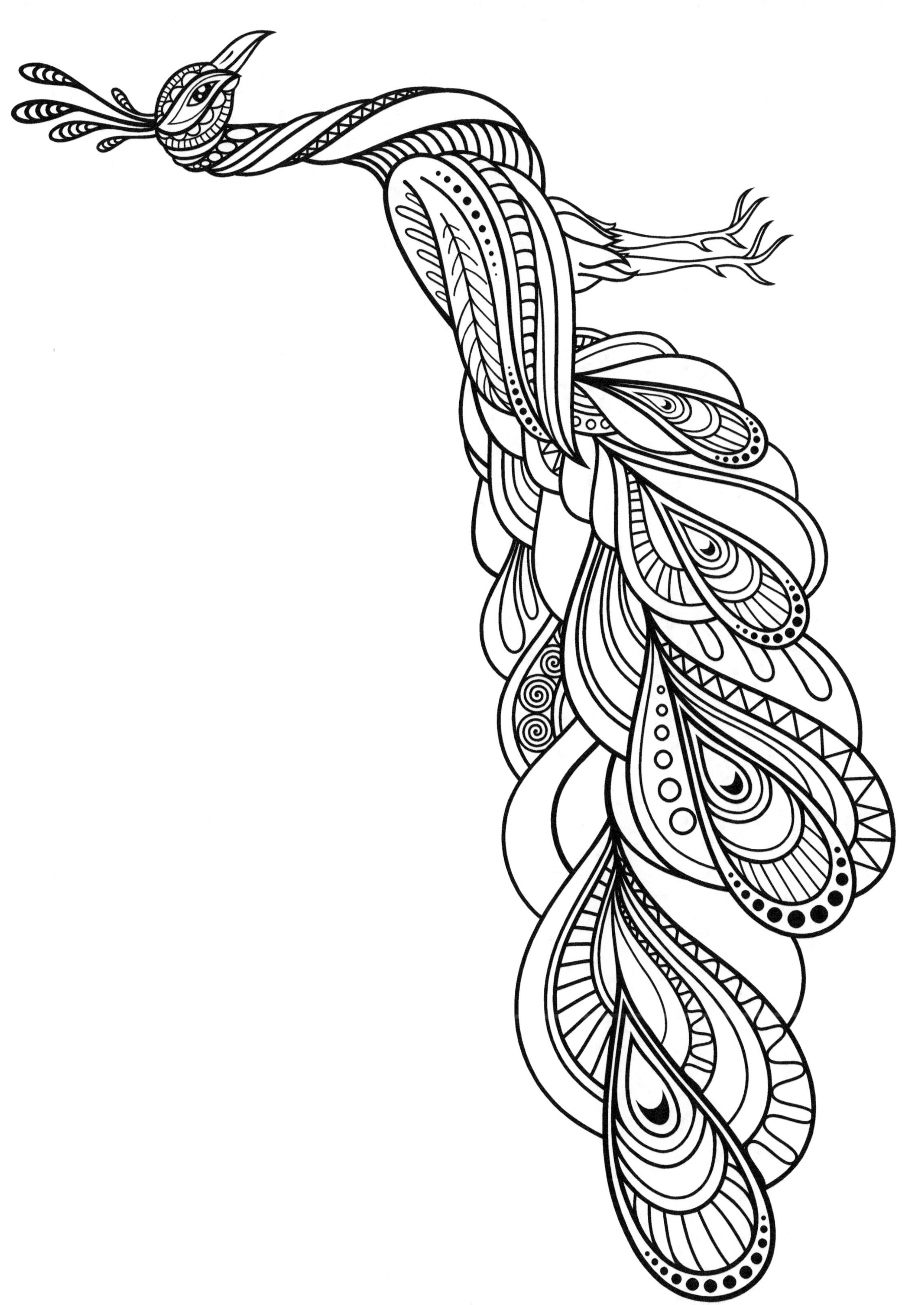

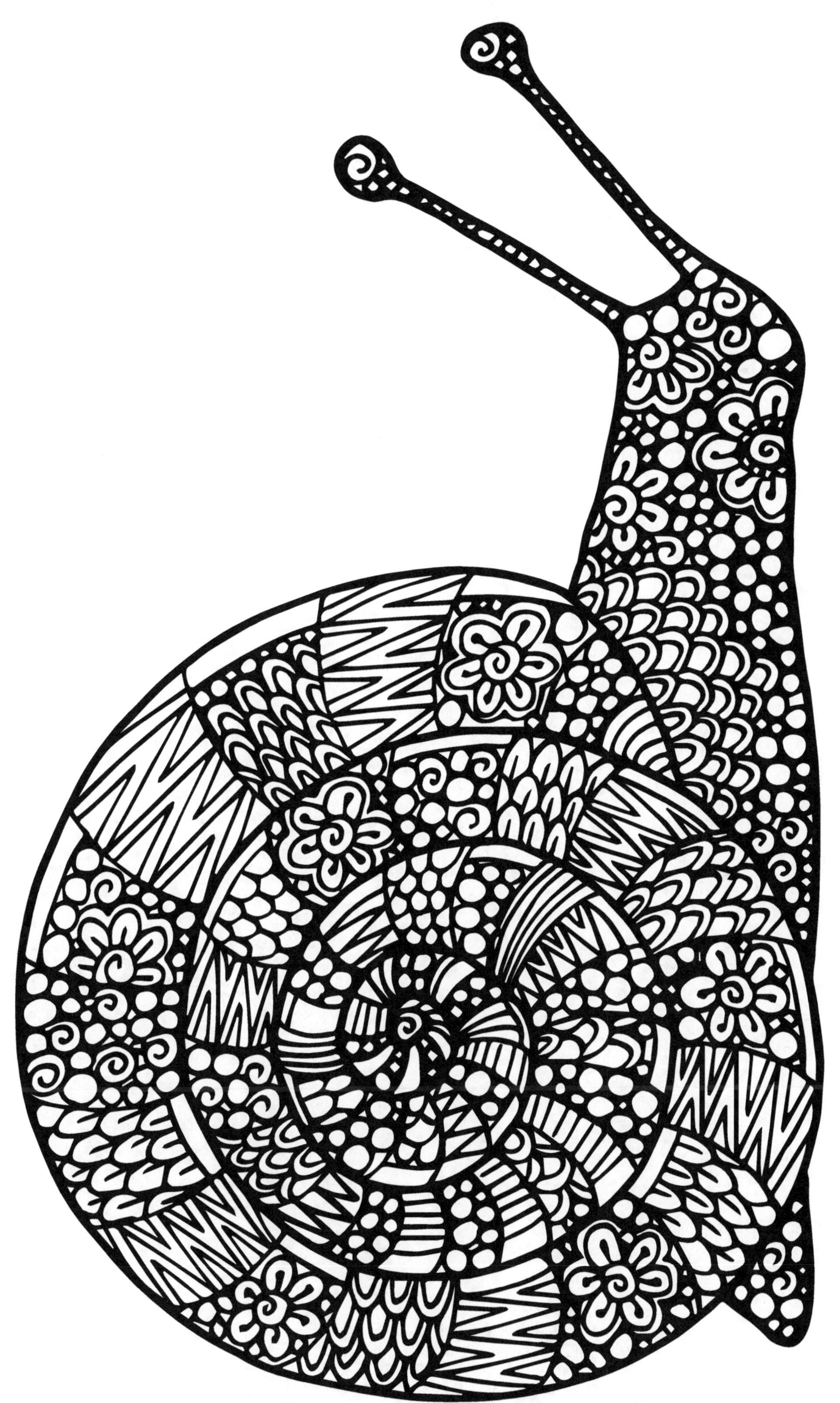

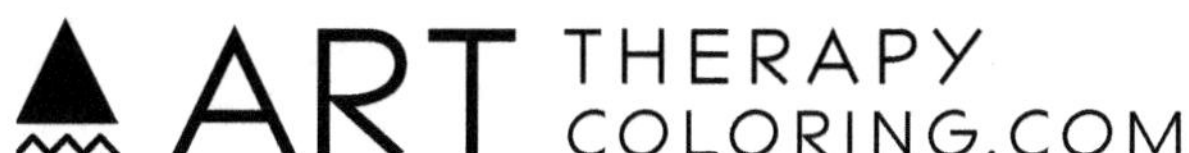

Test Your Colors

Drawings

Drawings

More By ART THERAPY COLORING.COM

Best Selling Art Therapy Coloring Books

Coloring Books For Adults:

- Zombie Coloring Book: Black Background
- Butterfly Coloring Book For Adults: Black Background
- Tattoo Coloring Book: Black Background
- Coloring Books for Adults Relaxation: Native American Inspired Designs
- Fishing Coloring Book for Adults: Black Background

Coloring Books For Men:

- Coloring Book for Men: Anti-Stress Designs Vol 1
- Coloring Book For Men: Fishing Designs
- Coloring Book For Men: Tattoo Designs
- Coloring Books for Men: Hunting
- Coloring Book For Men: Biker Designs

Coloring Books For Seniors:

- Coloring Book For Seniors: Nature Designs Vol 1
- Coloring Book For Seniors: Anti-Stress Designs Vol 1
- Coloring Books for Seniors: Relaxing Designs
- Coloring Book For Seniors: Floral Designs Vol 1
- Coloring Book For Seniors: Ocean Designs Vol 1

Coloring Books For Teens and Tweens:

- Coloring Books For Teens: Ocean Designs
- Coloring Books for Teen Girls Vol 1
- Teen Inspirational Coloring Books
- Coloring Book for Teens: Anti-Stress Designs Vol 1
- Tween Coloring Books For Girls: Cute Animals

Coloring Books For Kids:

- Horse Coloring Book For Girls
- Coloring Books For Boys: Sharks
- Coloring Books for Boys: Animal Designs
- Unicorn Coloring Book for Girls
- Detailed Coloring Books For Kids

Art Therapy Coloring Books

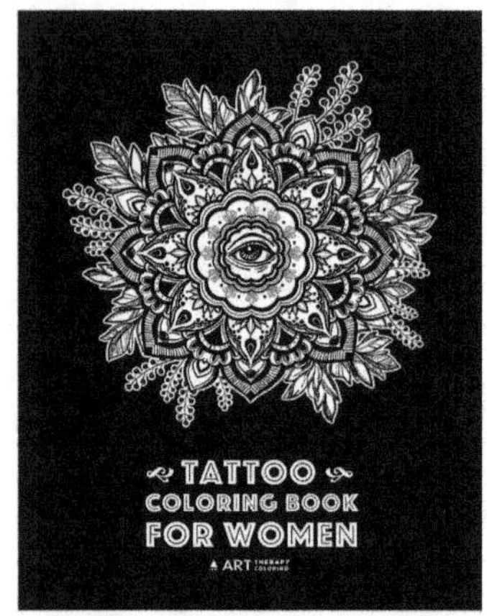

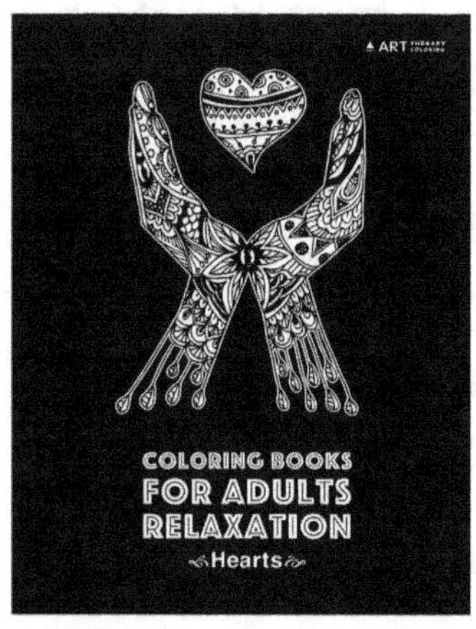

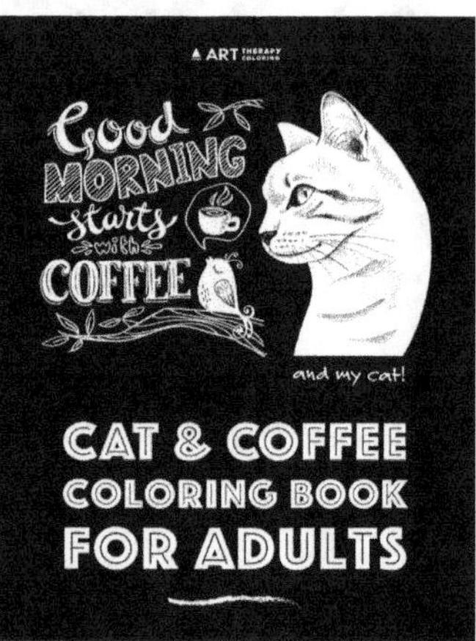

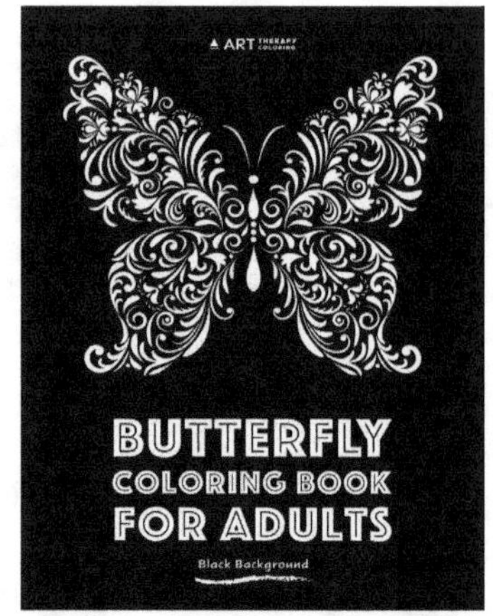

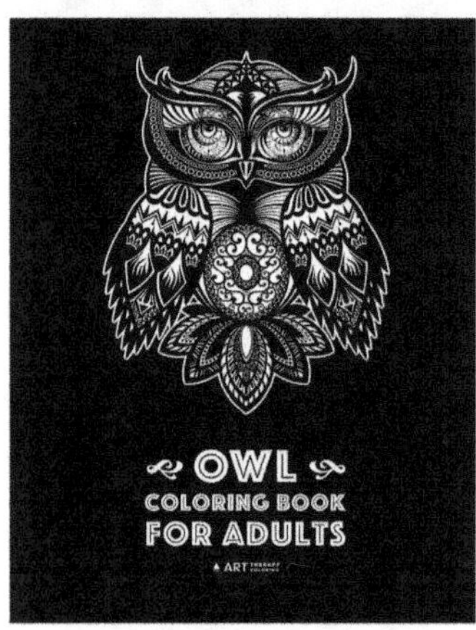

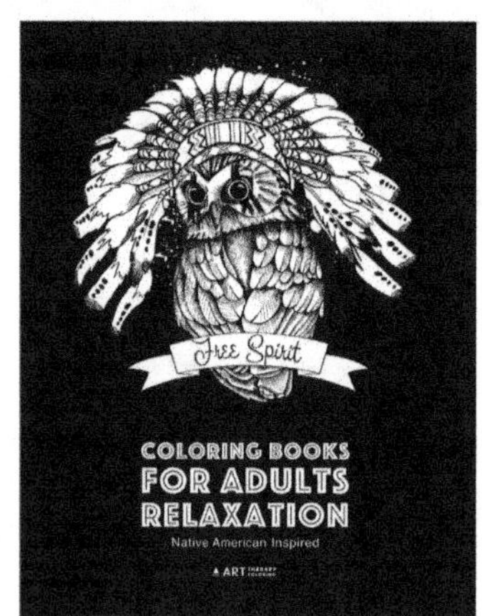

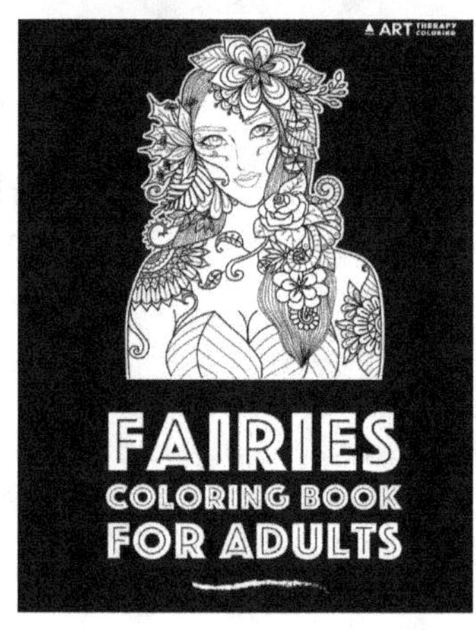

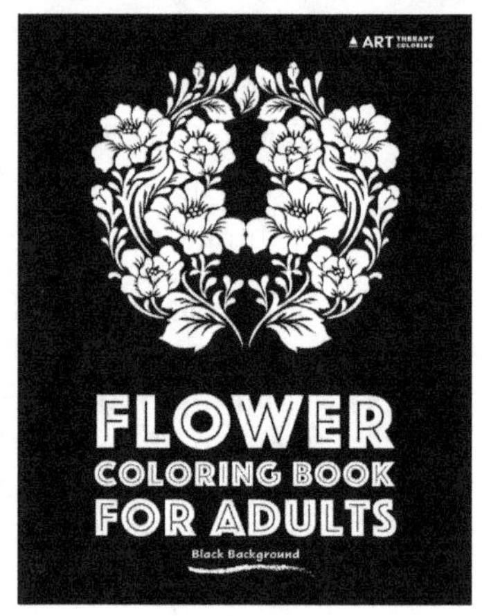

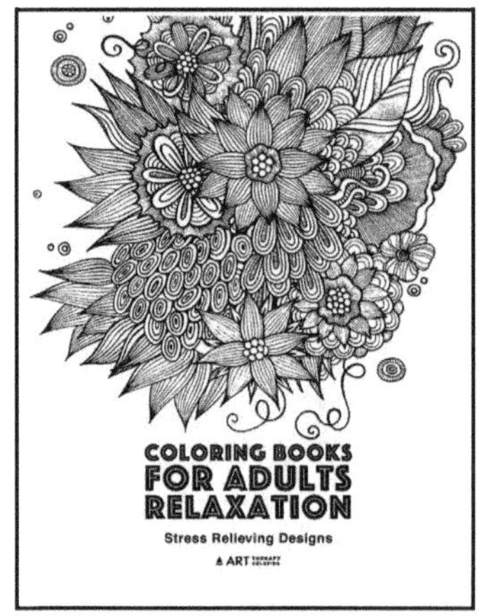

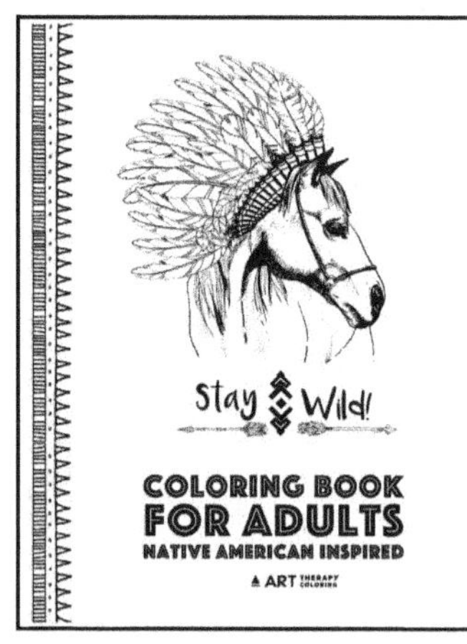

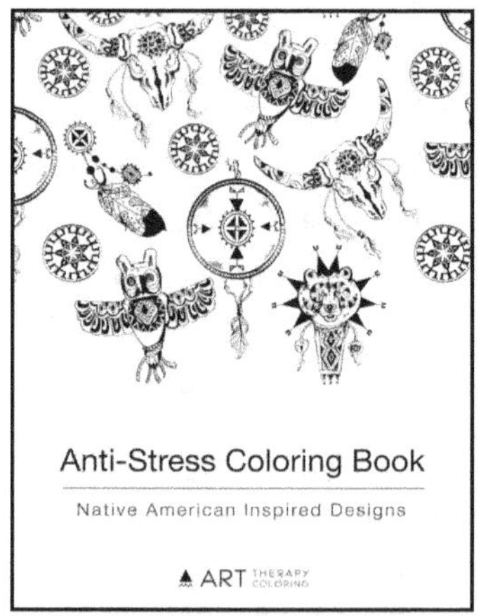

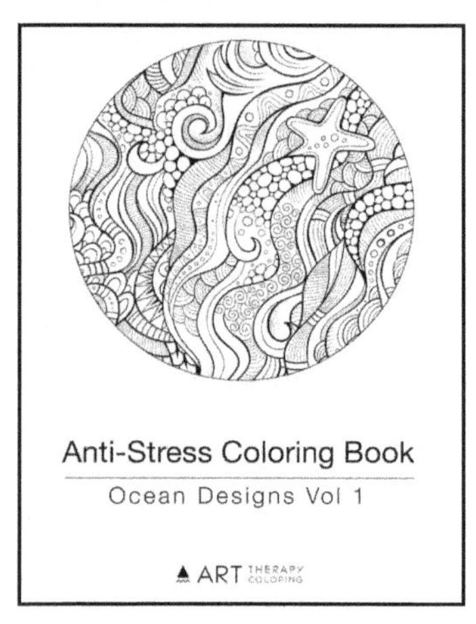

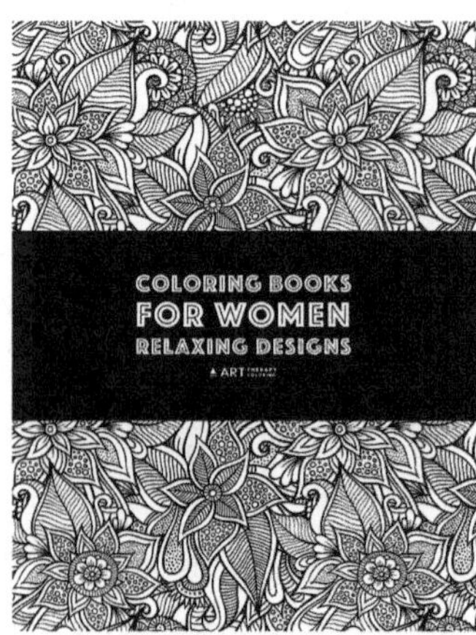

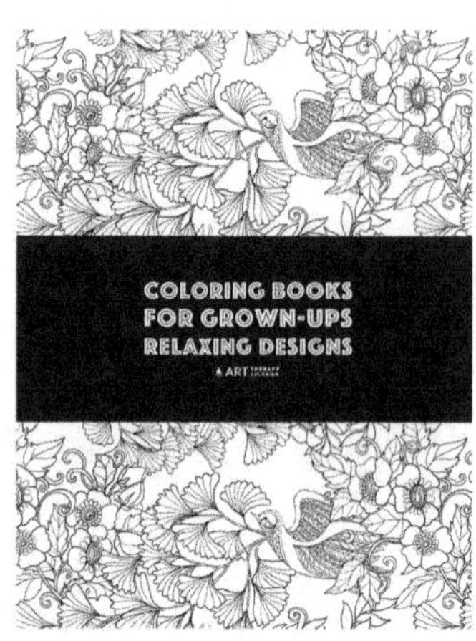

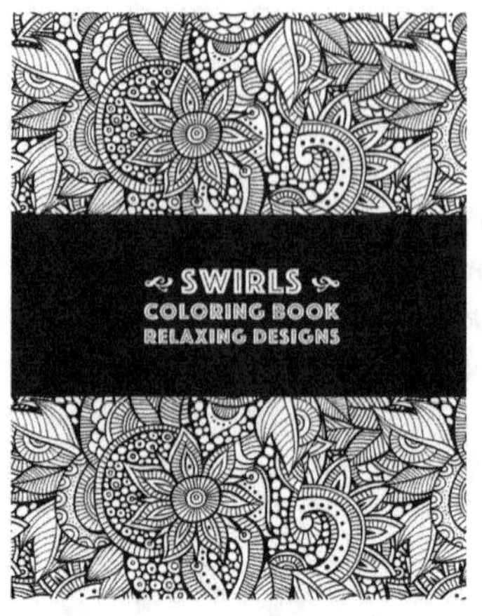

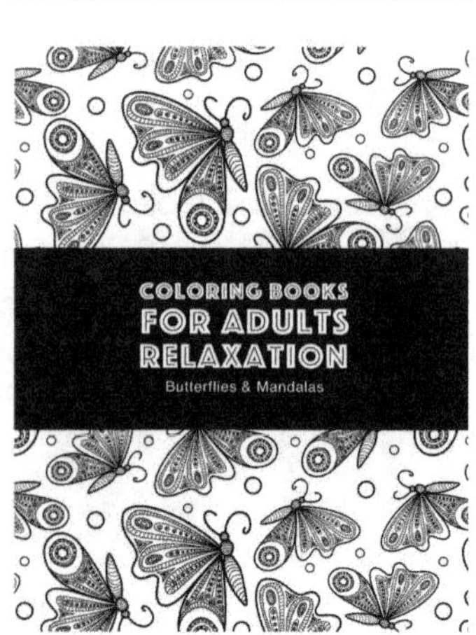

Art Therapy Coloring Books

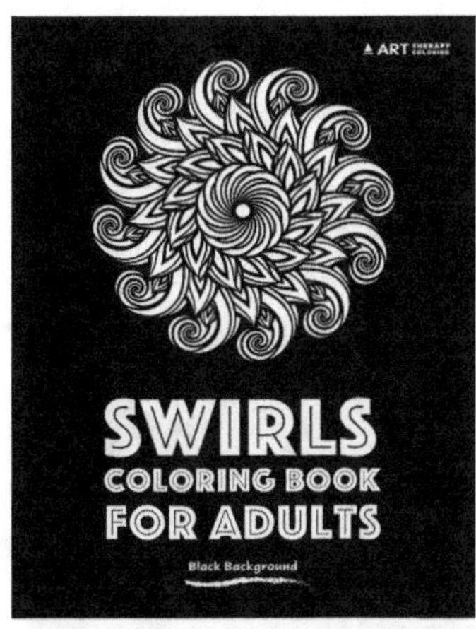

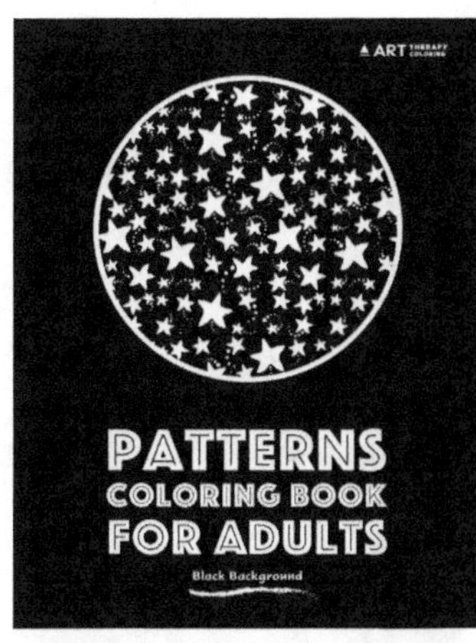

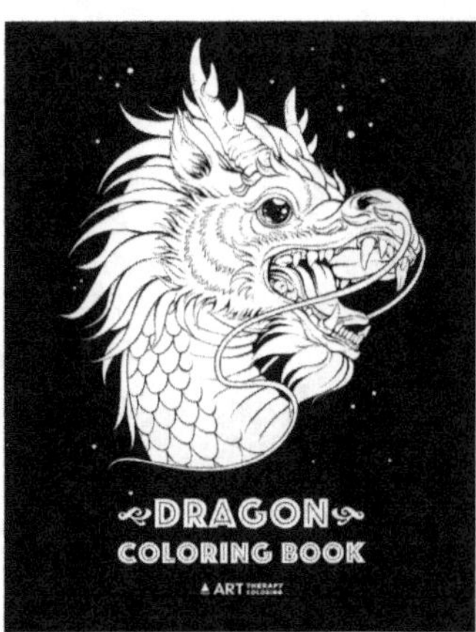

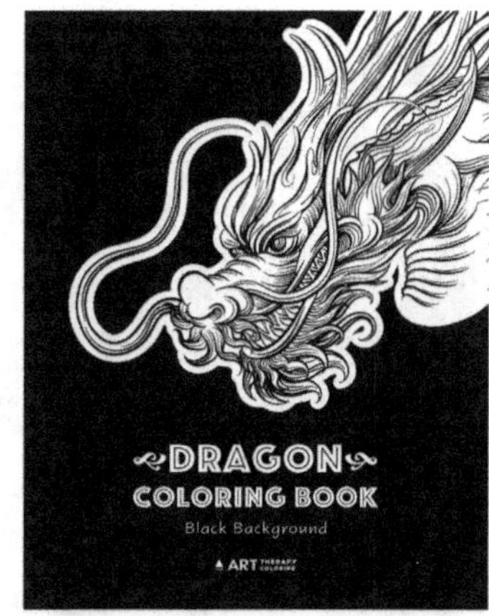

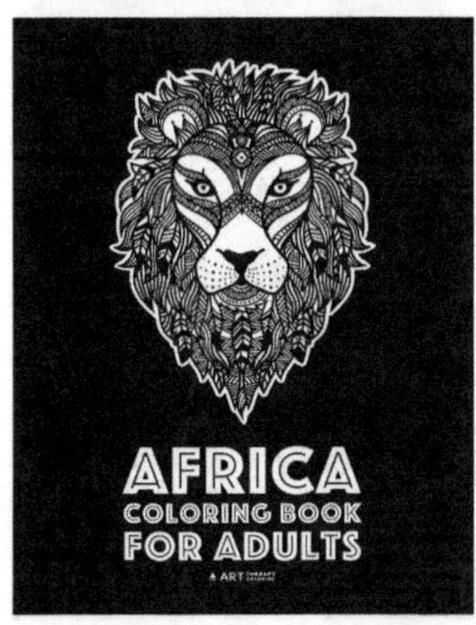

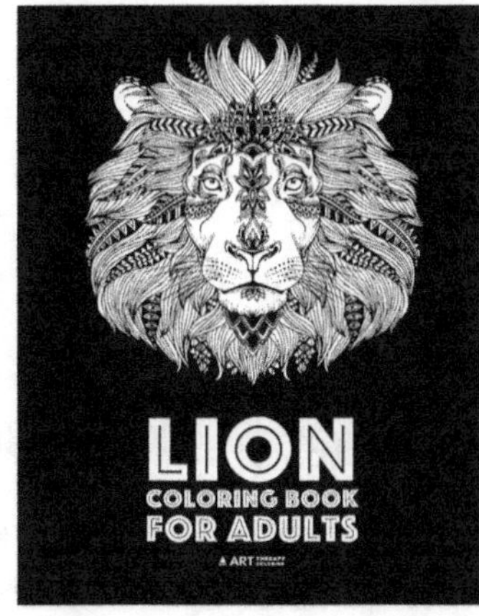

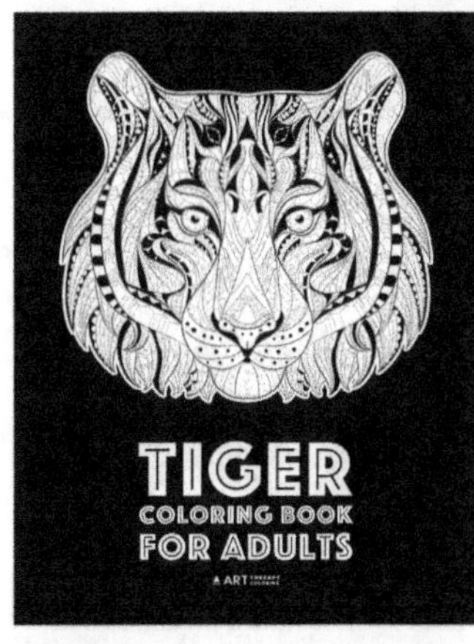

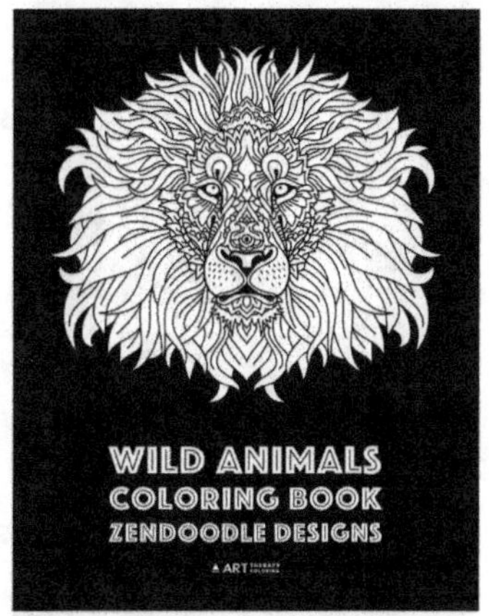

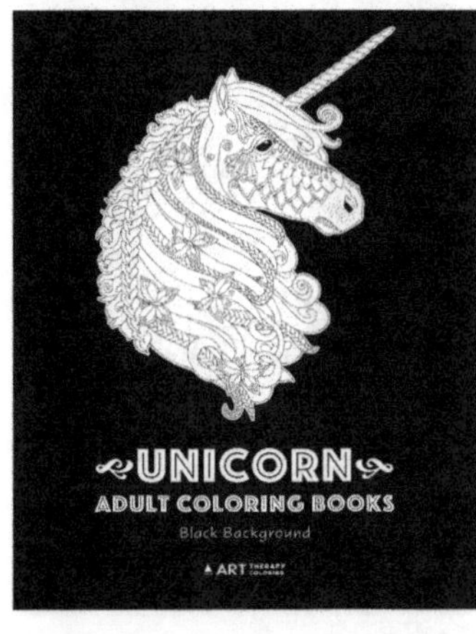

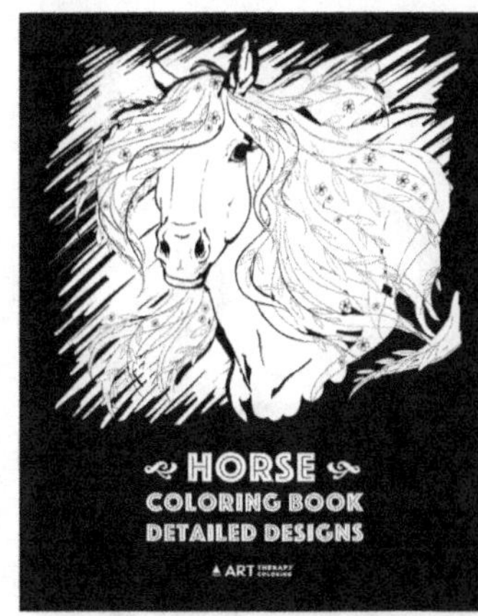

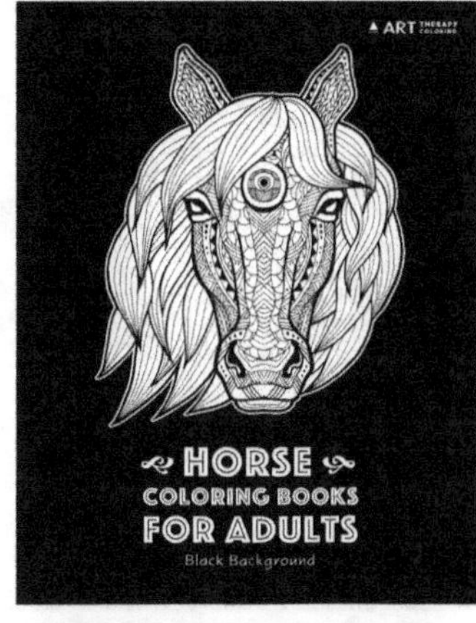

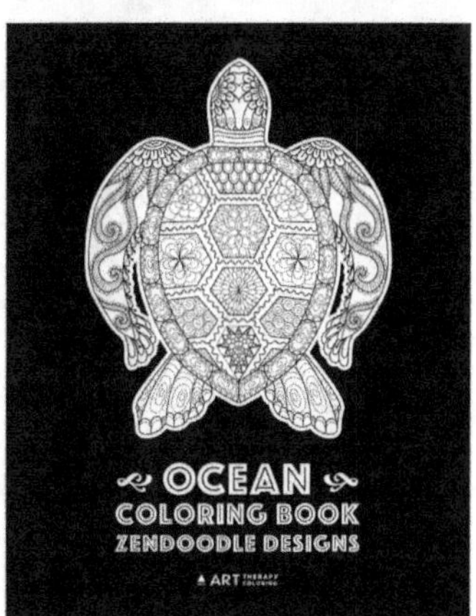

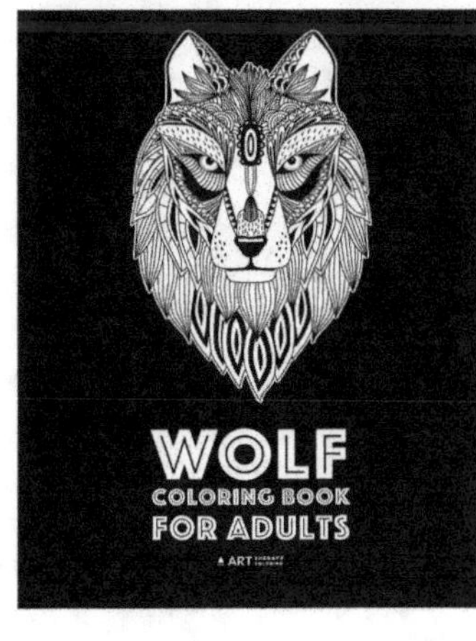

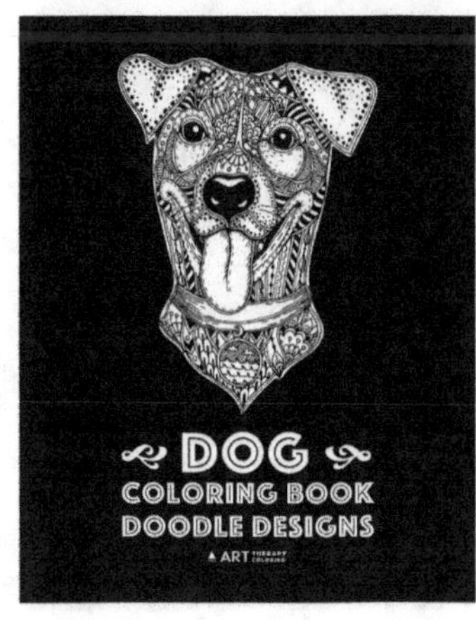

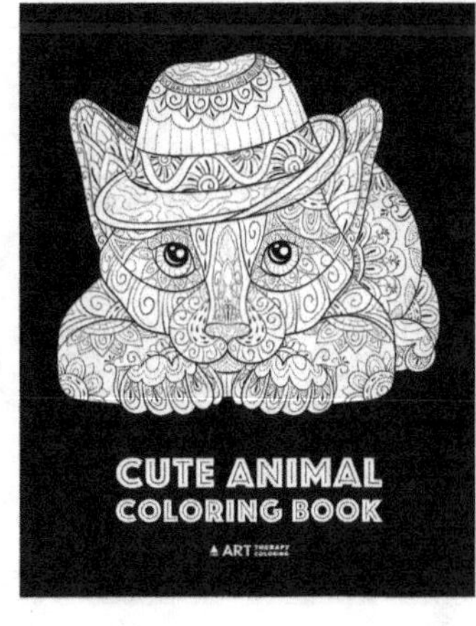

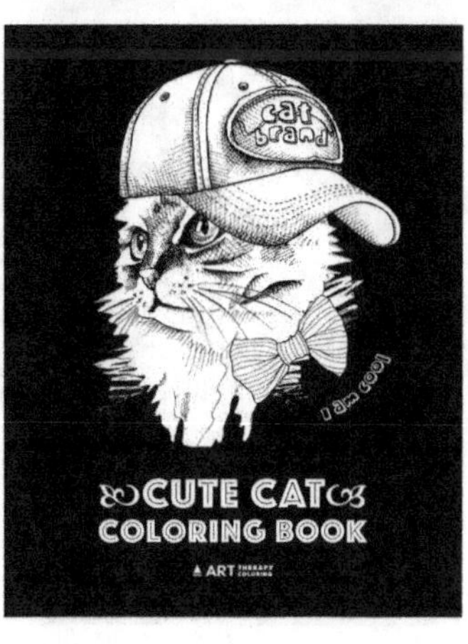

Art Therapy Coloring Books

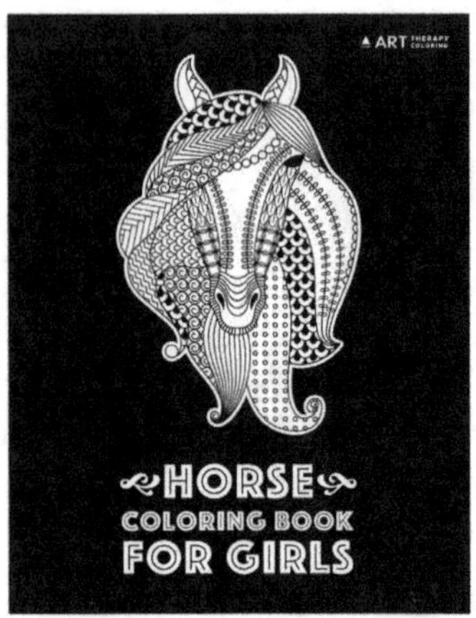

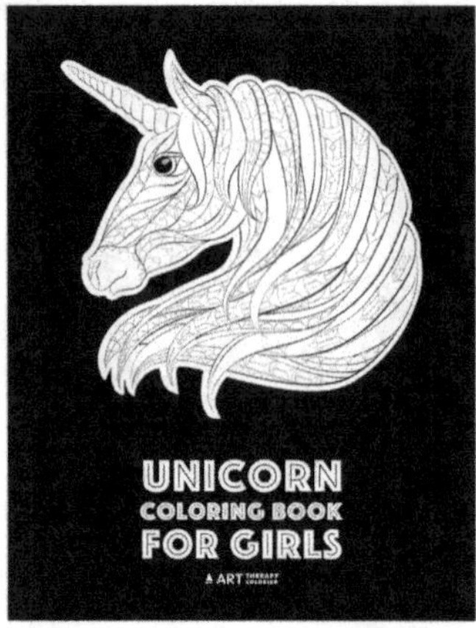

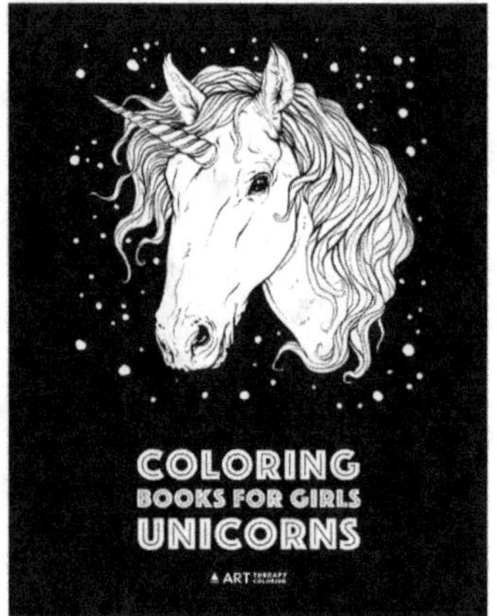

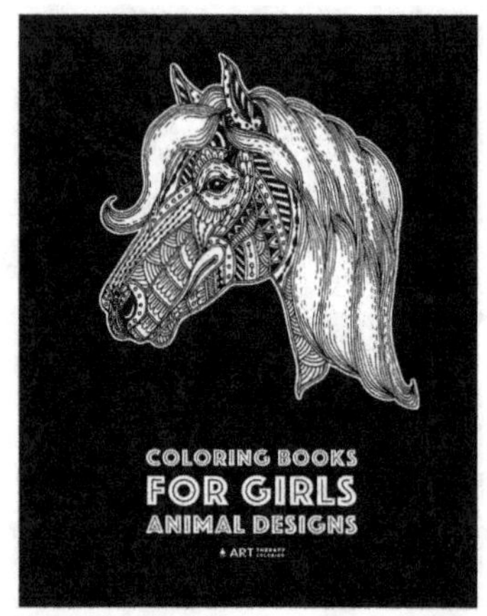

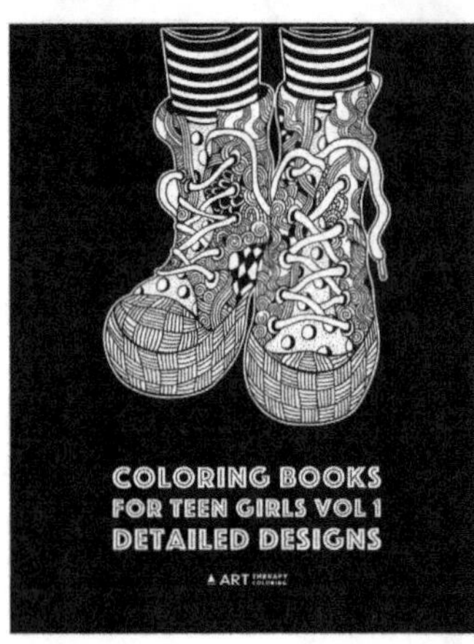

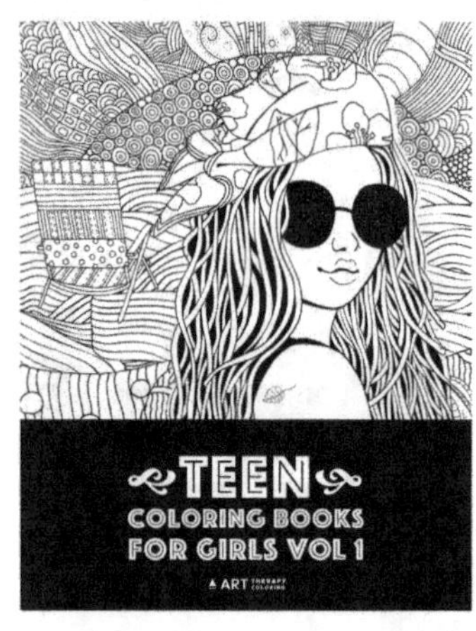

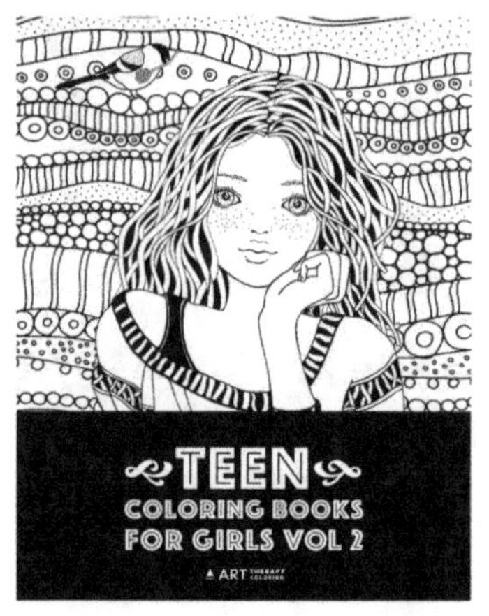

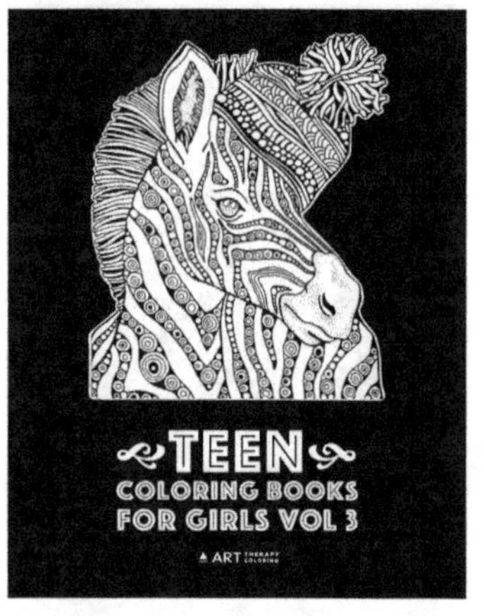

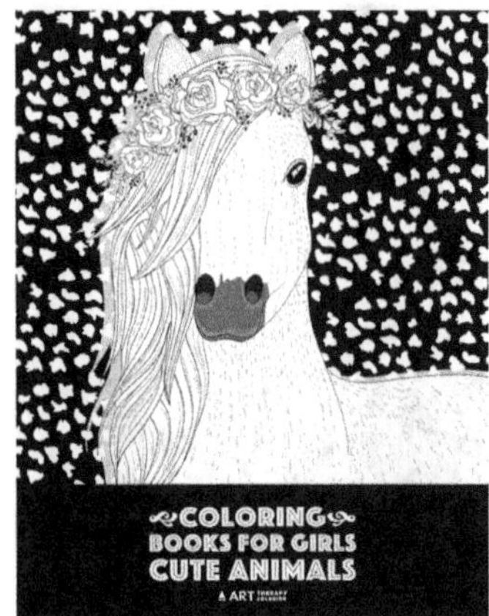

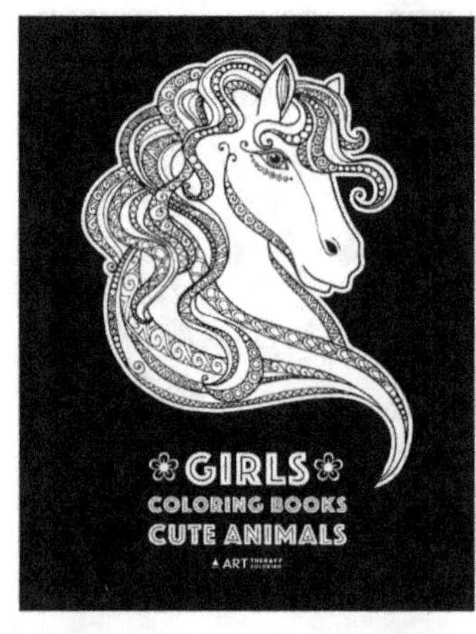

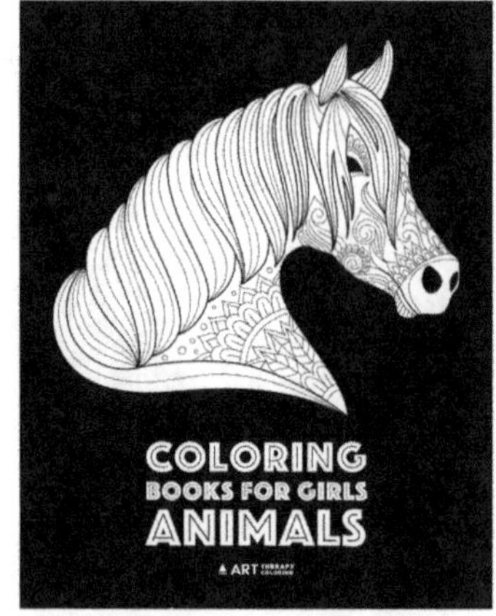

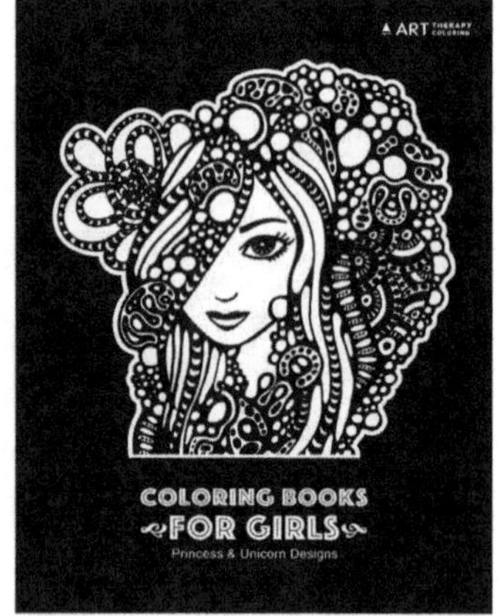

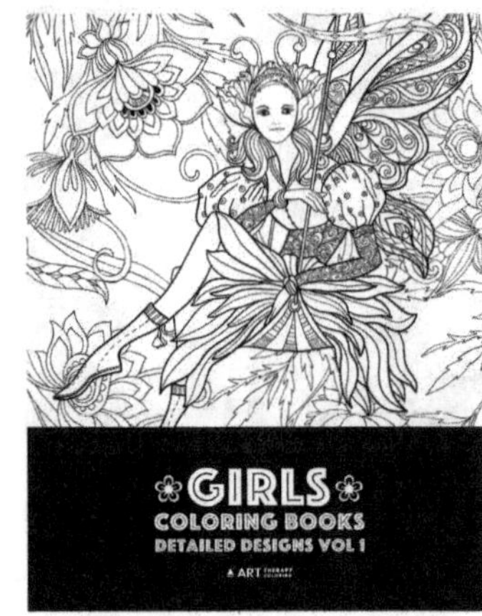

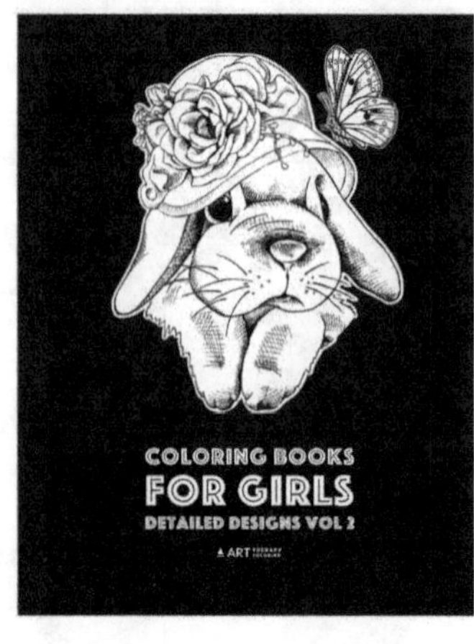

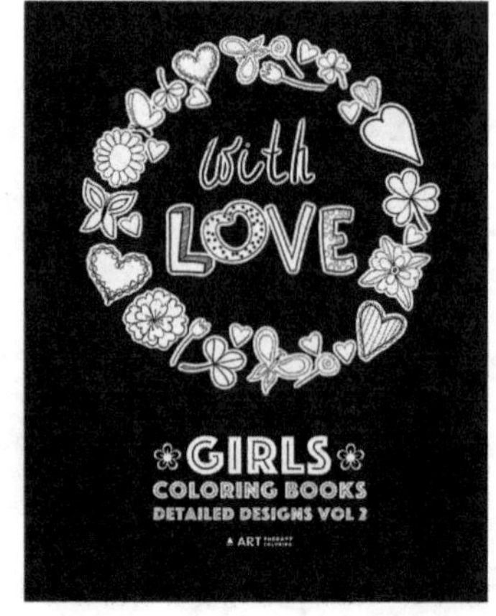

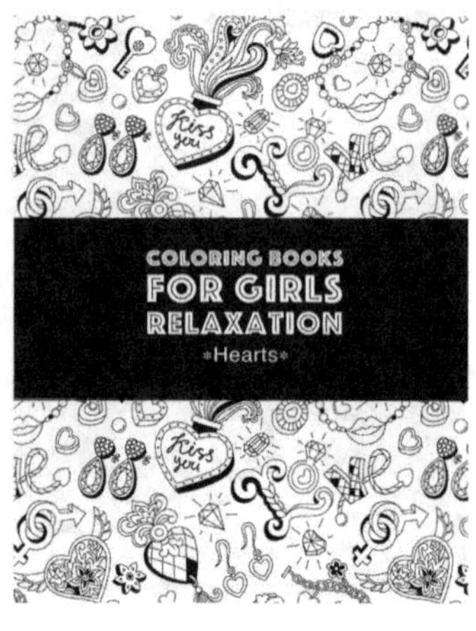

Art Therapy Coloring Books

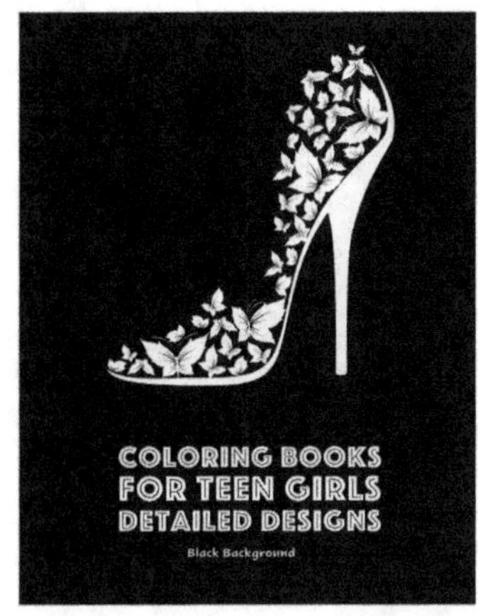

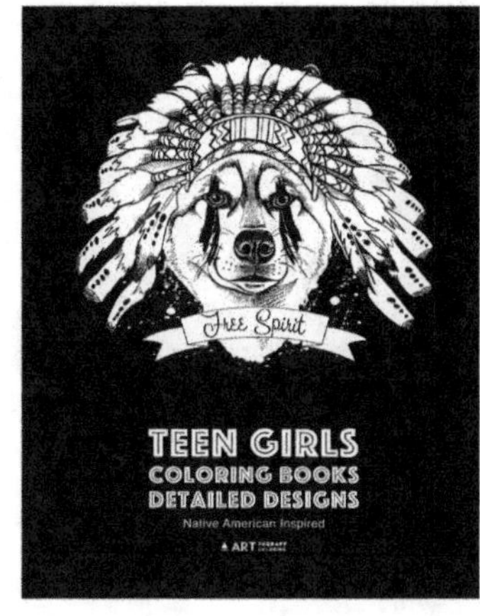

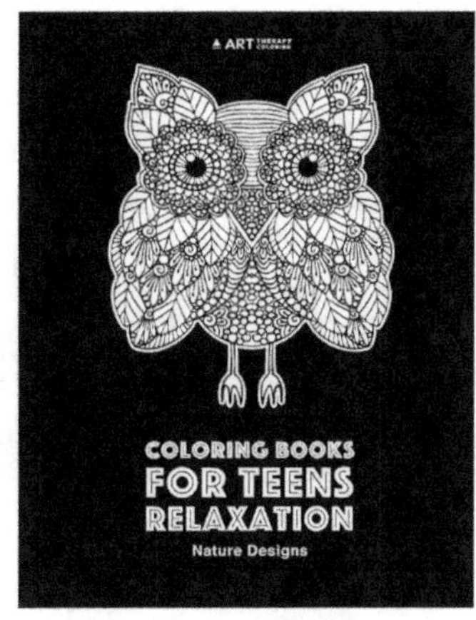

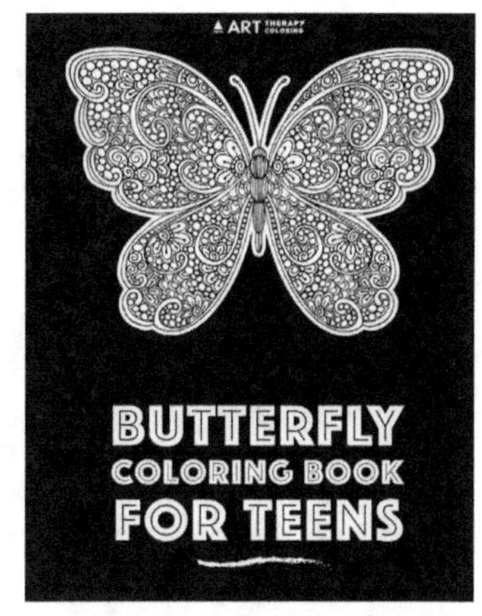

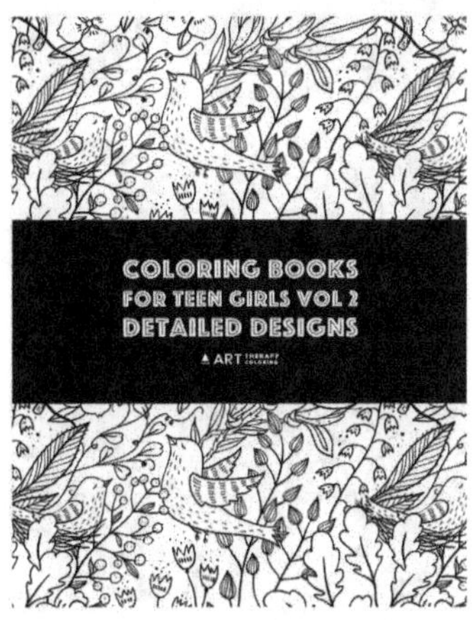

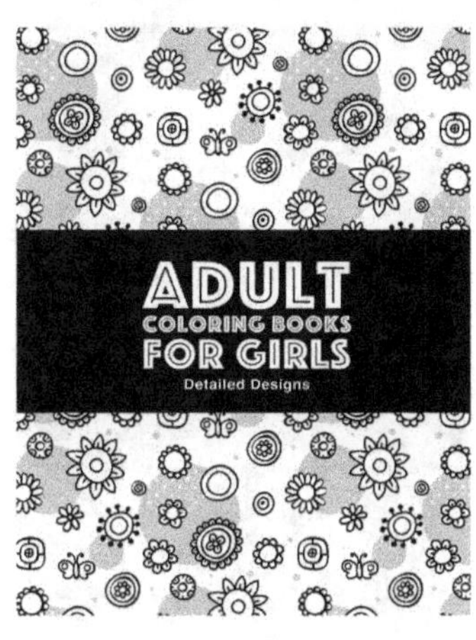

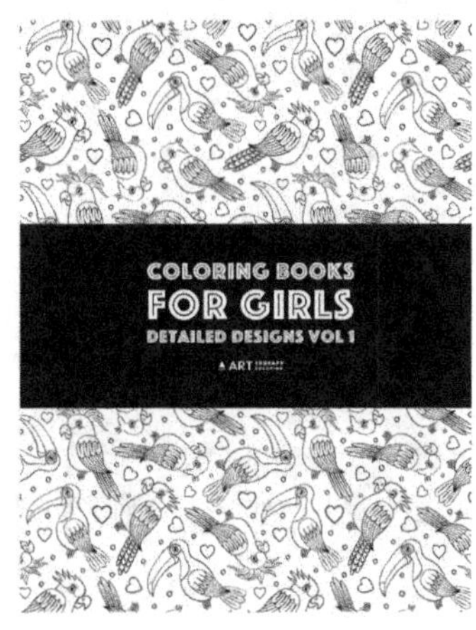

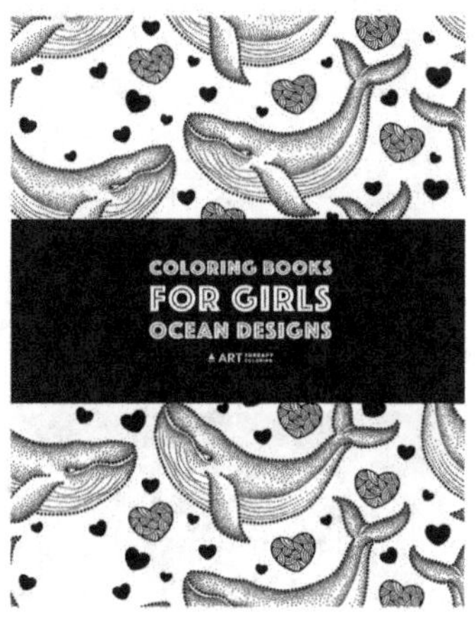

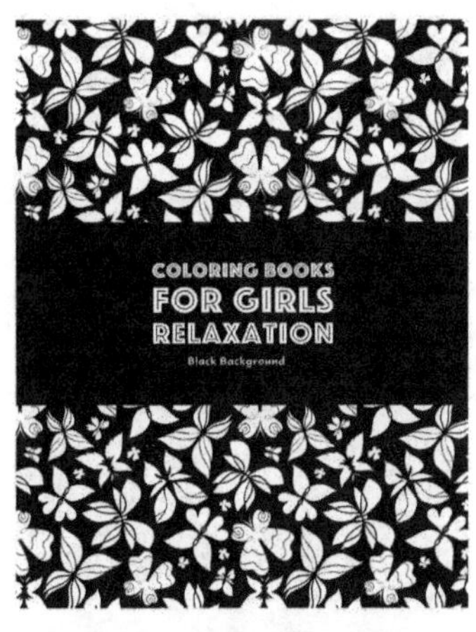

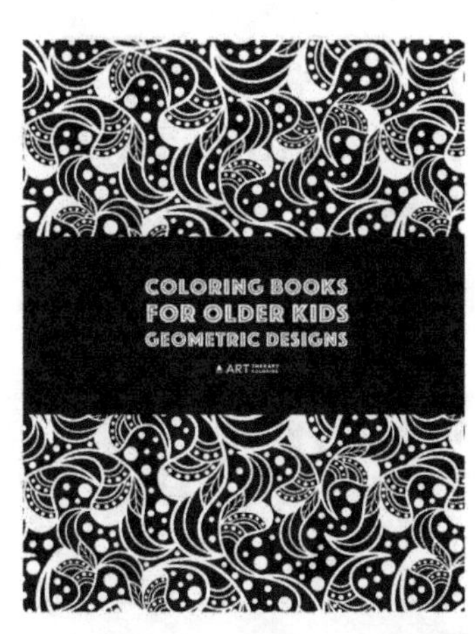

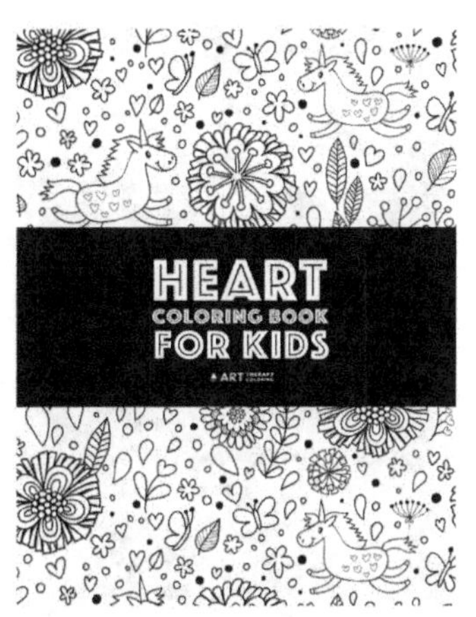

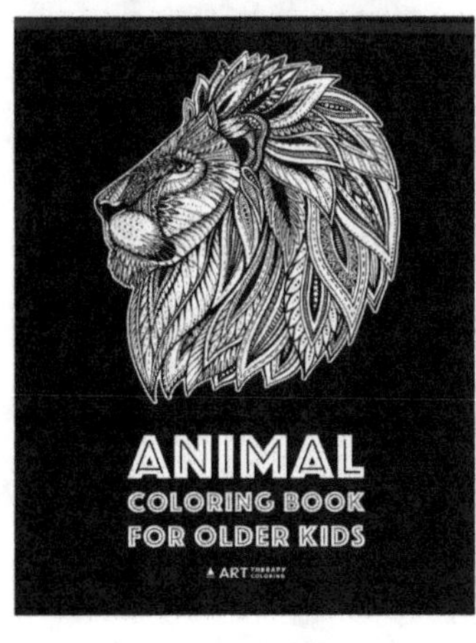

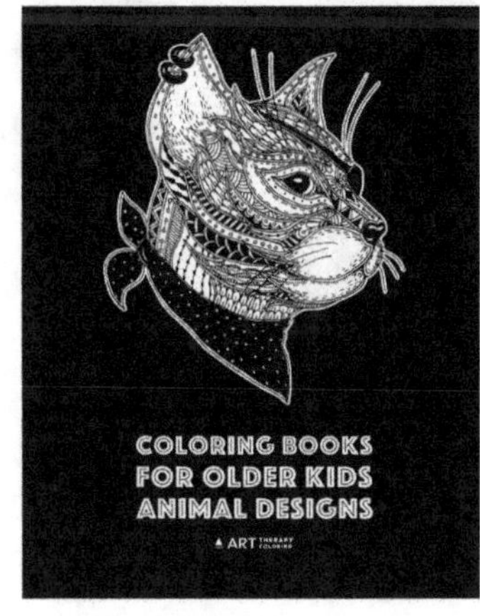

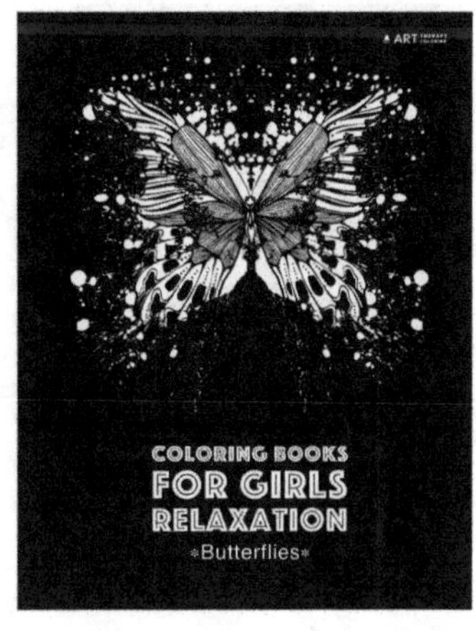

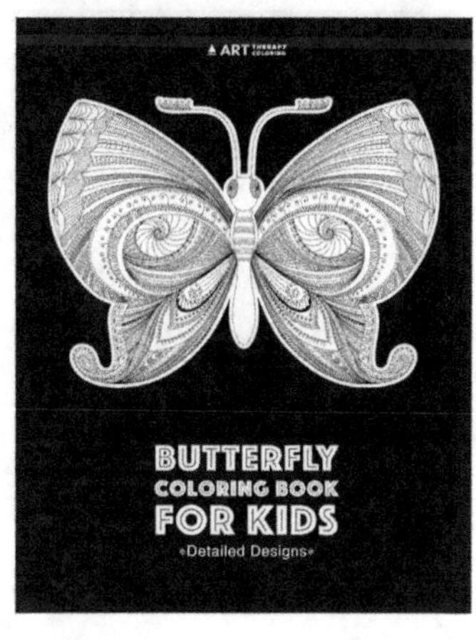

Art Therapy Coloring Books

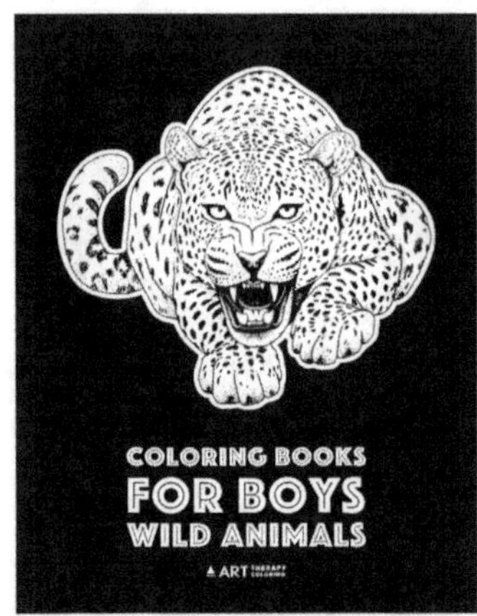
COLORING BOOKS
FOR BOYS
WILD ANIMALS
ART THERAPY COLORING

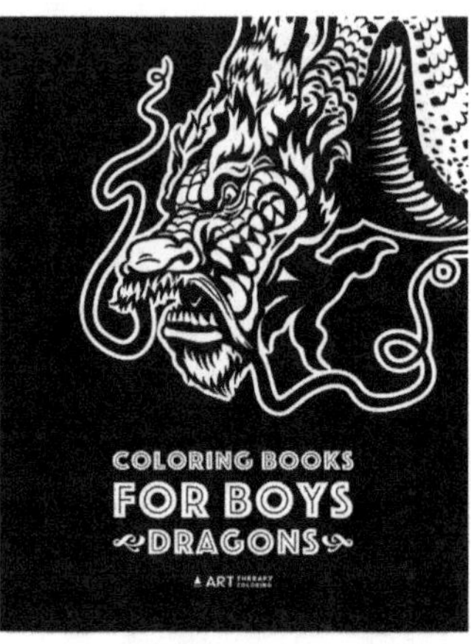
COLORING BOOKS
FOR BOYS
DRAGONS
ART THERAPY COLORING

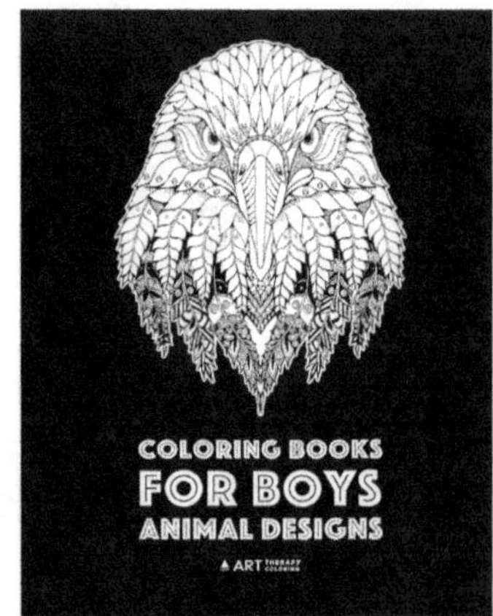
COLORING BOOKS
FOR BOYS
ANIMAL DESIGNS
ART THERAPY COLORING

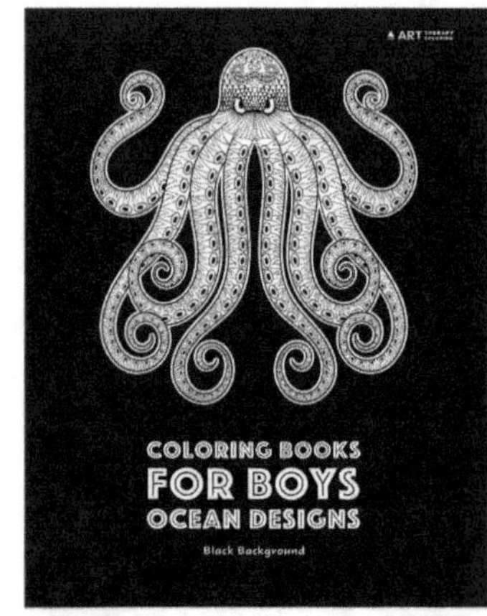
ART THERAPY COLORING
COLORING BOOKS
FOR BOYS
OCEAN DESIGNS
Black Background

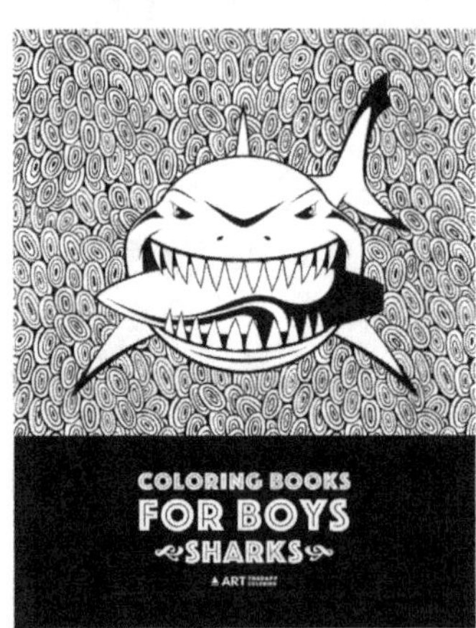
COLORING BOOKS
FOR BOYS
SHARKS
ART THERAPY COLORING

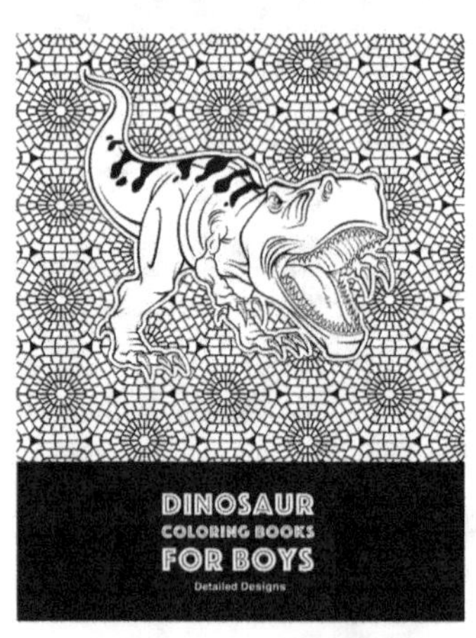
DINOSAUR
COLORING BOOKS
FOR BOYS
Detailed Designs

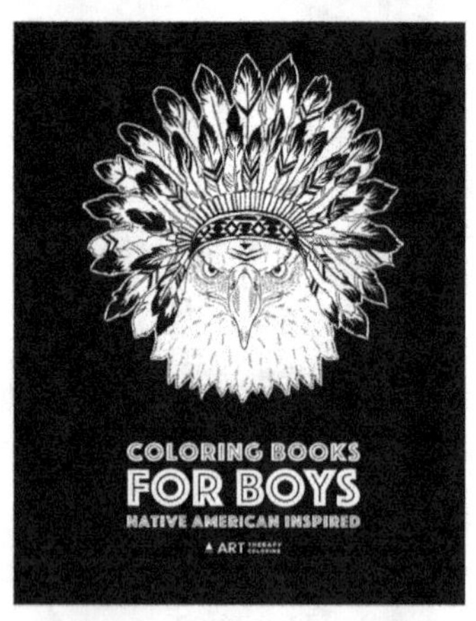
COLORING BOOKS
FOR BOYS
NATIVE AMERICAN INSPIRED
ART THERAPY COLORING

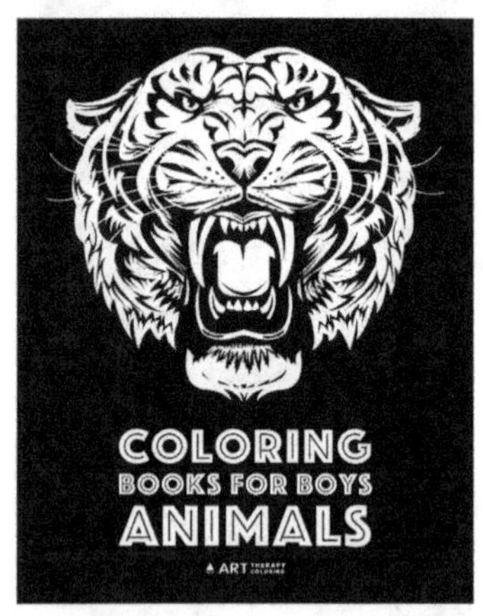
COLORING
BOOKS FOR BOYS
ANIMALS
ART THERAPY COLORING

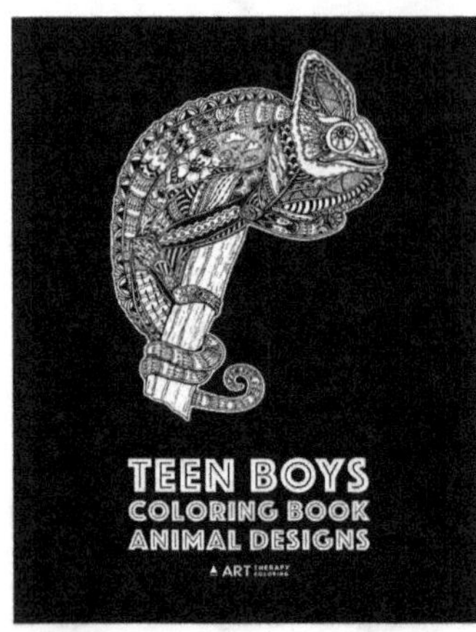
TEEN BOYS
COLORING BOOK
ANIMAL DESIGNS
ART THERAPY COLORING

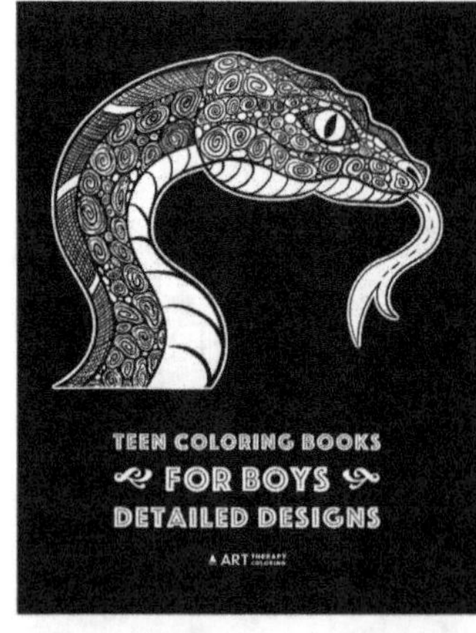
TEEN COLORING BOOKS
FOR BOYS
DETAILED DESIGNS
ART THERAPY COLORING

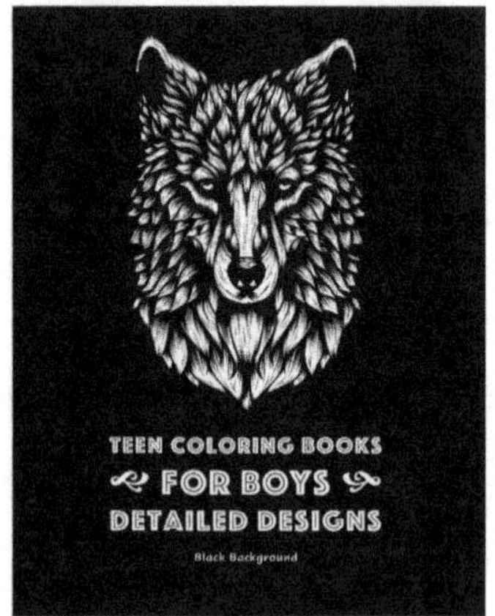
TEEN COLORING BOOKS
FOR BOYS
DETAILED DESIGNS
Black Background

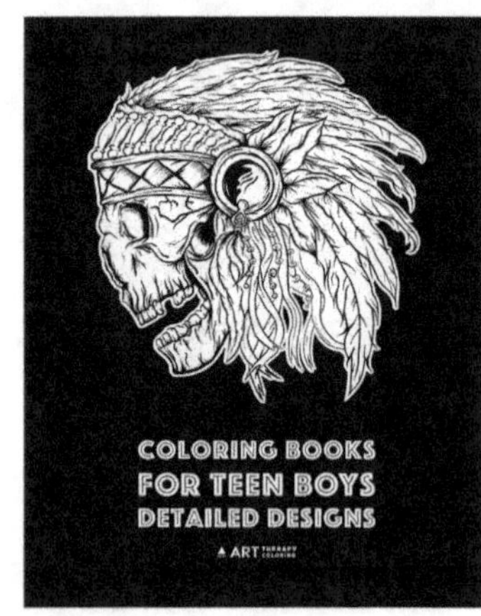
COLORING BOOKS
FOR TEEN BOYS
DETAILED DESIGNS
ART THERAPY COLORING

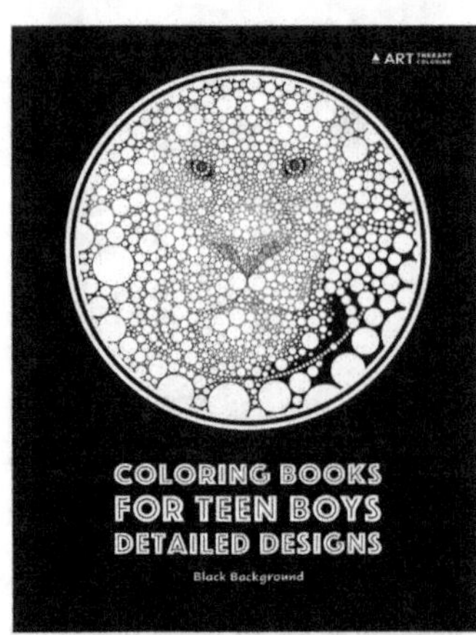
ART THERAPY COLORING
COLORING BOOKS
FOR TEEN BOYS
DETAILED DESIGNS
Black Background

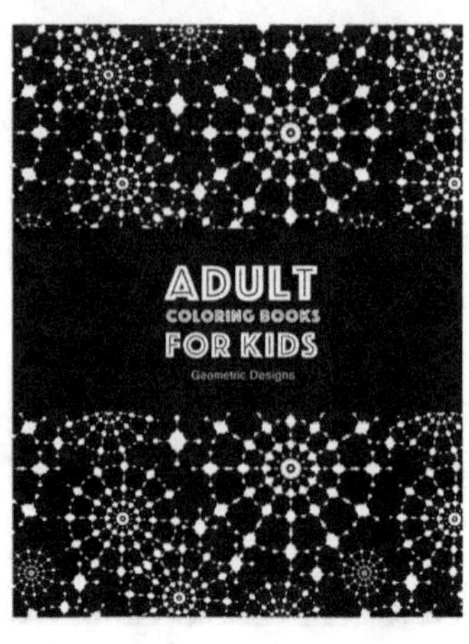
ADULT
COLORING BOOKS
FOR KIDS
Geometric Designs

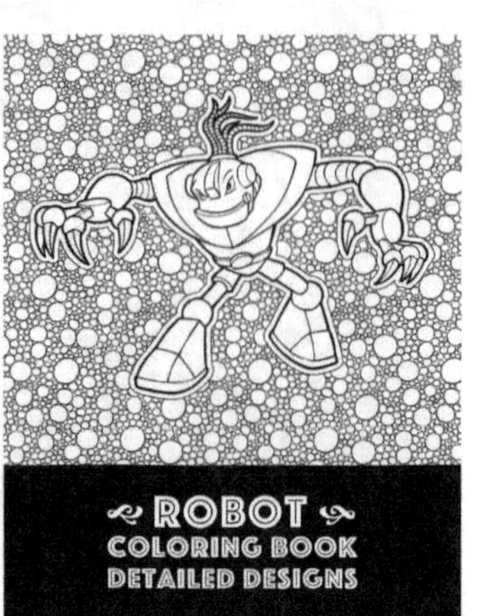
ROBOT
COLORING BOOK
DETAILED DESIGNS

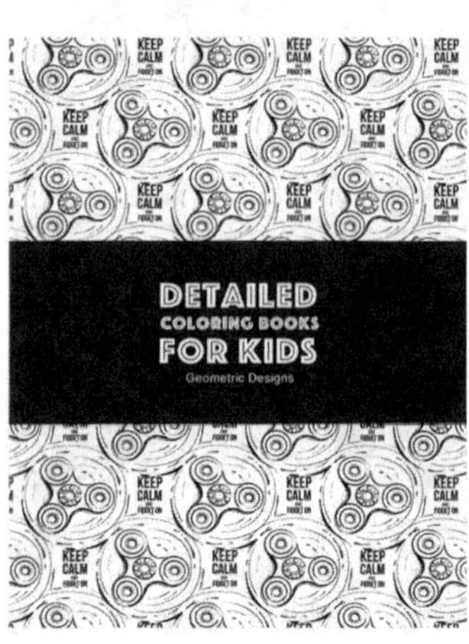
DETAILED
COLORING BOOKS
FOR KIDS
Geometric Designs

Art Therapy Coloring Books

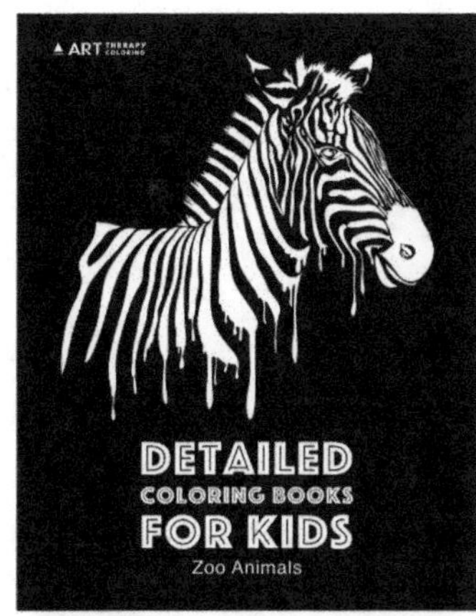

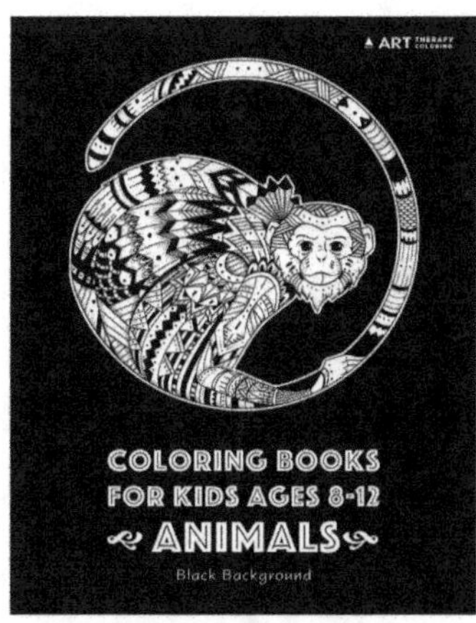

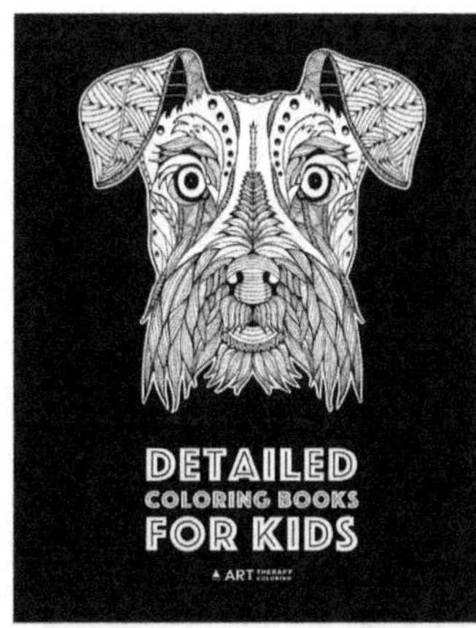

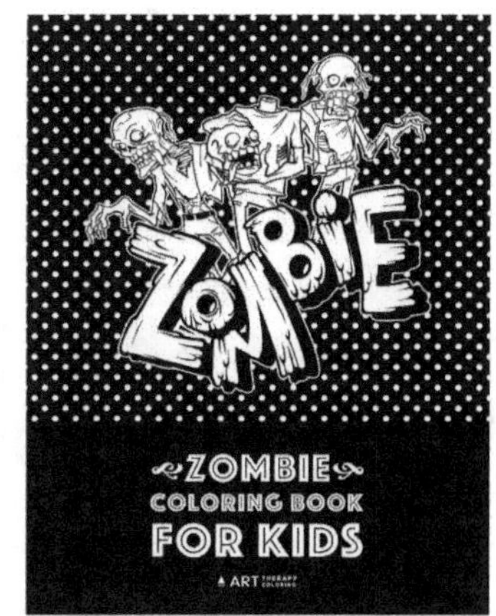

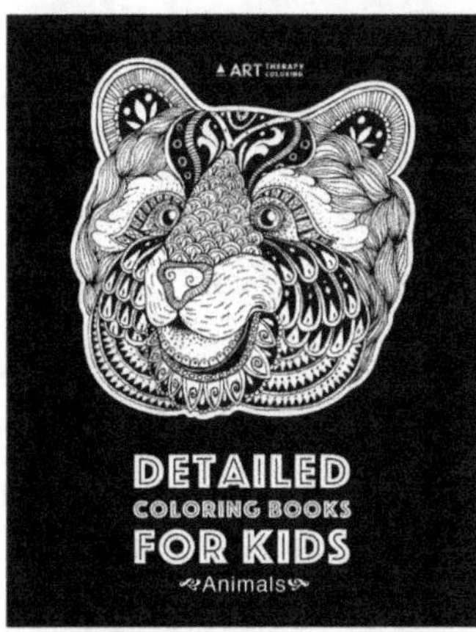

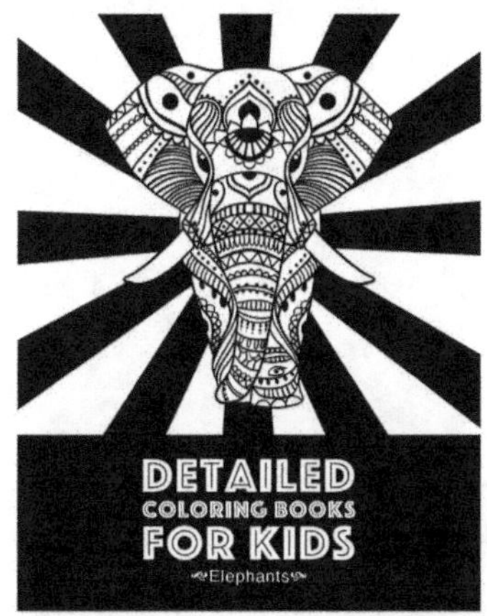

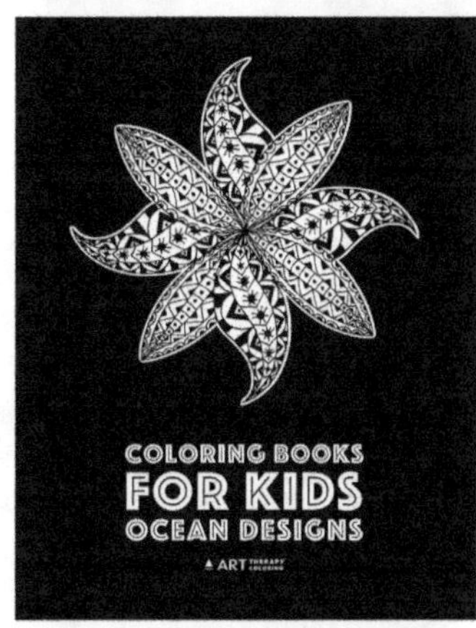

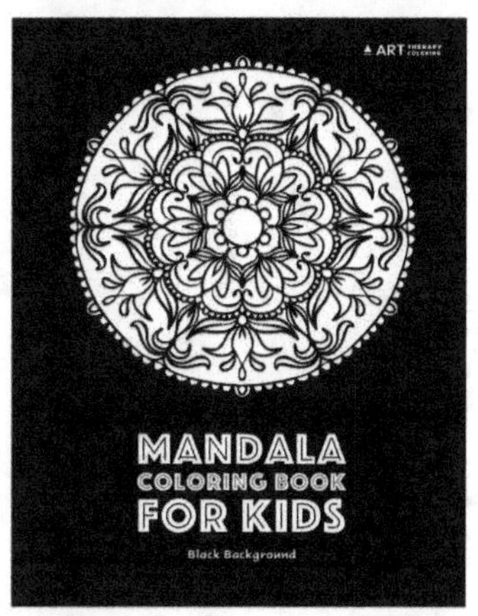

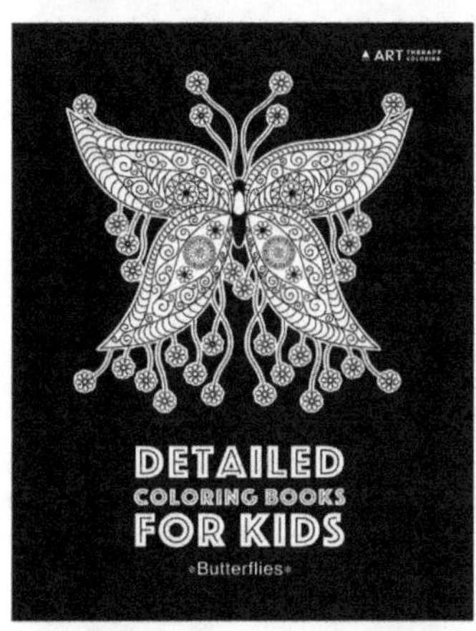

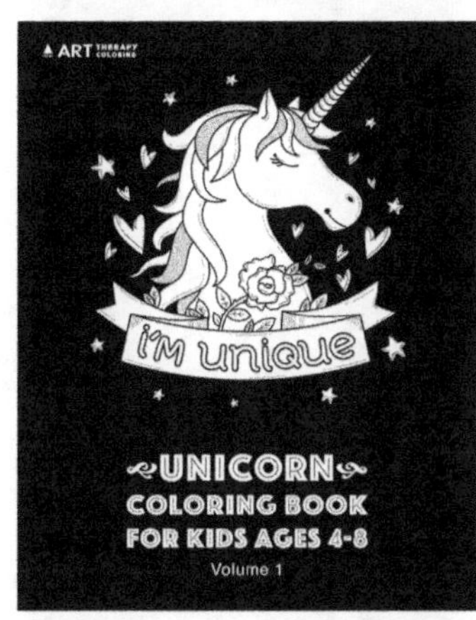

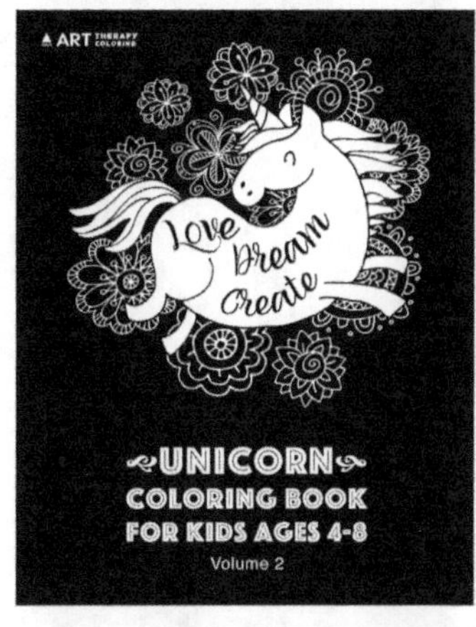

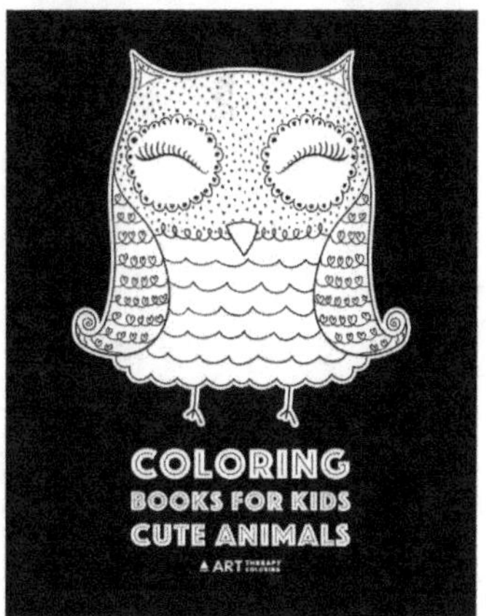

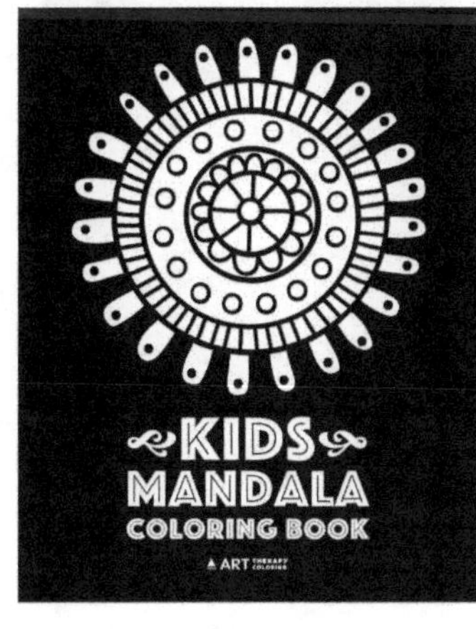

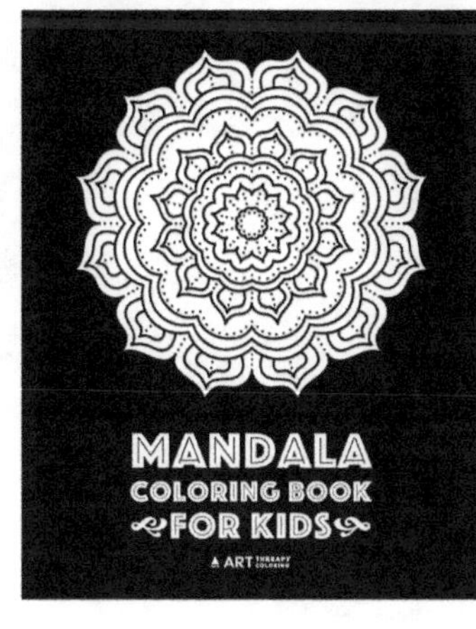

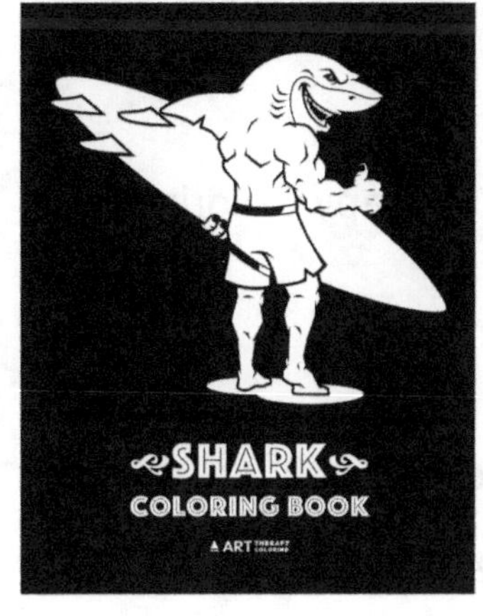

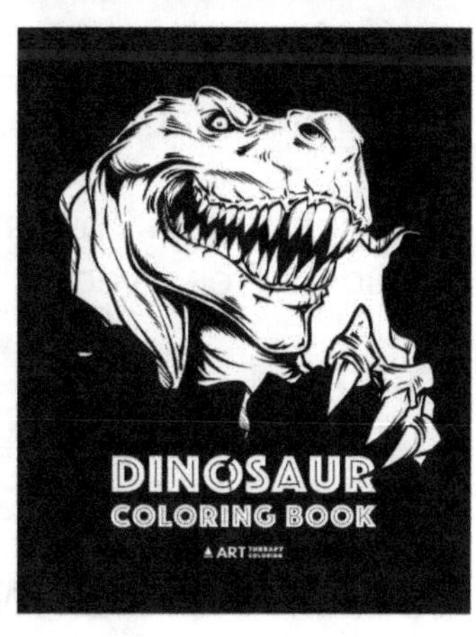

Anti-Stress Coloring Book
Nature Designs Vol 1

Published by:
Art Therapy Coloring
www.arttherapycoloring.com

ISBN: 978-1-944427-10-8

www.ingramcontent.com/pod-product-compliance
Lightning Source LLC
LaVergne TN
LVHW080335110826
845155LV00027B/245
* 9 7 8 1 9 4 4 4 2 7 1 0 8 *